WITHDRAWN

D1272313

QUEST FOR MYTH

QUEST
FOR MYTH

398
C386qr

BY

RICHARD CHASE

GREENWOOD PRESS, PUBLISHERS
NEW YORK

Copyright © 1949 by Louisiana State University Press

Reprinted with the permission
of Louisiana State University Press

First Greenwood Reprinting 1969

SBN 8371-2150-7

PRINTED IN UNITED STATES OF AMERICA

FOREWORD

AN INTEREST in the creative literature of our century forces upon us an interest in myth.

In fiction and poetry the prestige of naturalism, aestheticism, and symbolism has declined, for though the first and third, at least, are still usable disciplines, neither of them appears to be able to foster a first-rate literature. In the twenties and thirties our writers began to strive for a larger, a more arduous but a more promising achievement; a mythological literature. Yeats was devoted to the pursuit of myth—amongst the Irish folk, in the halls of Ireland's "big houses," in séances, and in dreams. In "Totem and Taboo" Freud created a poignant and compelling myth, a "scientific myth," as he called it, without which he apparently felt he could not adequately grasp the workings of the mind. Toynbee, our greatest historian, turned to myth at what he called "the critical points" of his *Study of History,* having found that the scientific method was unable to measure the profound realities of the rise and fall of civilizations. In *Finnegans Wake* we find a grandiose and witty lexicon of myths.

Twenty-odd years ago T. S. Eliot, to whom modern criticism owes so much that is good, wrote in his review of *Ulysses* that "the mythical method" could make "the modern world possible for art." And he invoked the names of Joyce and Yeats as fellow discoverers. I should prefer to say that "the mythical method" can make "art possible for the modern world." Eliot appears to think that myth is a kind of ready-made construct which gives form and guidance to our understanding of life. I think that myth is something dynamic and operative and that it depends upon art rather than vice versa— that in fact it *is* art. Eliot has not written at length on myth. But it seems to me that in so far as his statement in the *Ulysses* review is

v

185785

his considered opinion it is consistently belied by his use of myth in his own poems.

Our time is not the first in which men of letters have turned to mythology. But in our day there is a general impression that we know more about myth, because of the achievements of anthropology and psychology, than was hitherto known. This is true, though I have been unable to find any book, old or new, which treats myth adequately. As Andrew Lang, one of the best mythologists of the last century, remarked, the history of mythological studies "is the history of rash, premature, and exclusive theories." The theories of myth which float vaguely through our contemporary books and literary journals still answer Lang's description. We still find the tacit assumption almost universally made (made by Lang, for that matter) that myth is a kind of philosophy or science which tries to explain the universe or construct a world view. Even those who habitually talk of myth and science as if they were direct opposites (a nearly meaningless formulation) often make the same assumption. For they tell us, according to their persuasion, that myth is a higher kind of science or that it is a mistaken science. But myth has no more and no less to do with science than the "Ode to the West Wind," and no more or less to do with philosophy than "Ash Wednesday."

Other misleading ideas about myth are abroad. The *psychoanalysts* tell us that a myth is a collocation of sex symbols and is little different from a dream. The *semanticists* take myth to be a kind of curious intellectual puzzle involving the shuffling about of signs and symbols—an activity alleged to occupy both the waking and sleeping hours of children and "primitive men." The *apologists of religion* reduce myth to dogma or a system of rationalized belief which they tell us must be established before we can hope to create a new poetry and a new culture.

The central premise of this book is that *myth is literature and therefore a matter of aesthetic experience and the imagination,* a truth that literary critics should have affirmed long ago. The first critical step toward an understanding of mythological literature is to rescue myth from those who see in it only the means and ends of philosophy, religious dogma, psychoanalysis, or semantics. It is my hope that the present study takes this step.

The *anthropologists* have been trying for years—unsuccessfully—
to deliver the study of myth over to the literary critics. They have
repeatedly asserted that myth is art. "It is ironic," writes Professor
Ruth Benedict, "that the academic study of folklore should have
labored through its course under the incubus of theories explaining
seven-headed monsters and magic swords as survivals of primordial
conditions, allegories of the sun and moon or of the sex act or
etiological philosophizing and have ignored the unconfined role of
the human imagination in the creation of mythology." [1]

Let me say here that in this book I try not to raise the vexed question of the individual *vs.* society. But the question cannot be avoided
entirely. It seems to me that if we are to talk about literature and
myth, or literature *as* myth, we must think of myth primarily as the
aesthetic activity of a man's mind—not primarily as a cultural
phenomenon. It is for others to hold that a story or a world view
becomes mythical only when it is accepted by a whole people.

The present book does not pretend to be a complete statement
about myth. My purpose is to perform some of the spadework which
the current interest in myth appears to call for—by bringing certain of the older students of myth, mainly philosophers, historians,
philologists, psychologists, and anthropologists, into the proper perspective. My own tentative conclusions about myth emerge as the
book proceeds, becoming as explicit as I can make them in the last
three chapters. And in the last chapter I try to suggest at some length
a theory of poetry as myth by examining certain poems of Donne,
Wordsworth, Yeats, and Auden. But the book is only one contribution to a large cultural project, to which other kinds of contribution
might be made: for example, detailed studies of the mythologies of
individual peoples and tribes.

As a history of opinion the book obviously does not aim at being
exhaustive.[2] It is, rather, a selective handbook of opinion. Most of
the authors I have placed under discussion were chosen because they
appeared to have something enlightening to say or because they
made mistakes which must be described in order to be avoided. On
the other hand, I wished to convey to the reader the sensation that
he is reading a history, and in order to represent the flux and reflux
of opinion, I have discussed certain writers, such as Bayle, Voltaire,
Creuzer, and Max Müller, less because they are enlightening than

because they were typical or commanded great prestige in their times. I have furthermore provided a brief statement about the study of myth in antiquity.

It is a pleasure to be under obligation to Professor Emery Neff of Columbia University, who guided and encouraged me in the preparation of this book. I wish also sincerely to thank Professors Lionel Trilling and Jacques Barzun, who read the book in manuscript and offered me their helpful suggestions. And finally I wish to thank my wife, Frances W. Chase, for her heroic work with the manuscript and for various forms of assistance which, though they are too intangible, are yet too tangible to survive expression by the written word.

R. C.

Connecticut College
April, 1948

ACKNOWLEDGMENT

GRATEFUL acknowledgment is hereby made to the following publishers and authors for permission to quote from works to which they hold copyright:

Appleton-Century-Crofts, Inc., *Primitive Man as Philosopher* by Paul Radin and *Anthropology* by A. A. Goldenweiser.

The Macmillan Company, *Race, Language and Culture* by Franz Boas, copyright 1940 by Franz Boas; *The Golden Bough* by J. G. Frazer, abridged ed., copyright 1922 by The Macmillan Company; *The Tower* by W. B. Yeats, copyright 1928 by The Macmillan Company; *Later Poems* by W. B. Yeats, copyright 1924 by The Macmillan Company.

Viking Press and Paul Radin, *Primitive Religion* by Paul Radin.

D. C. Heath and Company, *General Anthropology* by Boas and others.

Oskar Piest, *God, Some Conversations*, ed. by F. H. Burkhardt.

The Dial Press and Philip Rahv, *The Great Short Novels of Henry James*, ed. by Philip Rahv.

Columbia University Press, *English Institute Annual, 1941*, and *English Institute Essays, 1947*.

Yale University Press, *Essay on Man* by Ernst Cassirer.

Houghton Mifflin Company, *Patterns of Culture* by Ruth Benedict, copyright 1934 by Ruth Benedict.

McGraw-Hill Book Company, Inc., *Social Anthropology* by Paul Radin, copyright 1932 by McGraw-Hill Book Company, Inc.

Alfred A. Knopf, *The Decline of the West* by Oswald Spengler.

Liveright Publishing Corporation, *Primitive Religion* by R. H. Lowie.

Harvard University Press, *Mythology and the Romantic Tradition*, 1937, by Douglas Bush and *Philosophy in a New Key*, 1942, by Susanne Langer.

Random House, *Basic Writings* by Sigmund Freud and *The Collected Poetry of W. H. Auden*.

CONTENTS

CHAPTER I

TRADITIONAL VIEWS
OF MYTH

THE ANCIENT world bequeathed to modern times certain ideas for the study of myth. No less than we, the Greeks and early Christians were fascinated by the bizarre creatures and the cryptic or terrible happenings which the myths of primitive times described. The writers of the ancient world, seeking to understand the myths of their ancestors out of intellectual curiosity or, perhaps oftener, out of a desire to reconcile the myths to a preconceived system of thought, developed three general views of myth: the allegorical-philosophical, the euhemeristic, the Christian-apologetic.

With the appearance of recorded philosophical thought in Greece came the conscious interpretation of mythology. The metaphysicians, as Grote says, were concerned to show that the gods and spirits of the old myths were really nothing but primitive versions of the new metaphysical concepts.[1] The moralists wished to show that the apparently silly or obscene stories of mythology were really didactic allegories. Early philosophers, such as Thales and Pythagoras, tried to show that the ancient myths were allegories of nature and that the mythical beings were personifications of natural phenomena. Oceanus, the nymphs, and Styx were interpreted as representing water, and the gods in general were reduced to the elements of nature. In various guises this venerable method of interpretation attained great prestige among students of myth in the nineteenth century.

The Stoics, concerned to justify their ethical and ascetic religion, attempted to raise the myths to the level of their own intellectual preoccupations.[2] Zeno, Cleanthes, and Chrysippus devoted themselves to this systematic purification of the savage past. Their method was also largely allegorical. They took the myths to be ingeniously symbolized concepts of the nature of the universe or beautiful veils concealing profound moral principles. Even the outrageous and obscure myths were treated as allegories containing abstruse knowledge. Zeus was said to be the universal principle, the "primary fire," or the "ether." The lesser gods were all parts of Zeus: Hera was the air; Hades, vapor; Hephaestus, fire; Demeter, earth. The Homeric story of Hephaestus' expulsion from heaven signified primitive men kindling their fires by means of lightning or sunbeams. The Stoics supposed that certain gods symbolized moral qualities: Ares was Rashness; Aphrodite, Profligacy; Leto, Forgetfulness. Even the heroes were moral essences: Hercules represented wisdom and the monsters he overcame were human passions.[3]

This allegorical method, given a new sanction by the copious allegorizing of the medieval poets and theologians, was taken up again by the Humanists of the Renaissance. The purpose of the Humanists was to salvage the pagan myths from the disrepute into which they had fallen, by showing—as the Greeks had before them —that the myths could be reconciled with the ideals of a civilized age. Boccaccio says in the Preface to *The Genealogy of the Gods* (1375), "these interpretations will enable you to see not only the art of the ancient poets, and the consanguinity and relations of the false gods, but certain natural truths, hidden with an art that will surprise you, together with the deeds and morality of the ancients, which are not a matter of everyday information." [4] In his *Mythologiae sive explicationum fabularum* (1551) Natale Conti sought to show that the Greek myths were only the doctrines of the great Greek philosophers in allegorical form. Francis Bacon himself in his *De Sapientia Veterum* (1609) demonstrated that Cassandra represented Plainness of Speech; Styx, Treaties; Pan, Nature; Daedalus, the Mechanic; and Dionysus, Desire. In Bacon's opinion the claws of the Sphinx were "the axioms and arguments of science" which "penetrate and hold fast the mind." The riddles of the Sphinx were of two kinds: one concerning physical, the other concerning human, nature.[5] And this, thinks Bacon, is the division into which the proper use of allegory shows the ancient myths to be divided.[6] It must be admitted that Bacon was not at his best as an interpreter of myths.

The allegorical method, as it was used by the Humanists and by the Greek philosophers, though profoundly misleading, had certain positive values: it asserted that myths must be taken seriously and it pleaded the continuity of history.

2.

Euhemerism is the theory that the gods are deified men who once lived on earth as conquerors, rulers, or renowned philosophers and that myth is history distorted by the fancy of storytellers. Euhemerus the Messenian (*c.* 330–*c.* 260 B.C.) wrote a book called *The Sacred Record,* in which he describes a journey he made to the island of "Panchaea" off the coast of Arabia. On Panchaea, says Euhemerus, is a temple of Zeus "erected by himself at the time when he reigned over the whole inhabited earth." [7] There is also a pillar with an inscription telling of the famous deeds of Ouranos, Kronos, and Zeus. From this inscription we learn that Zeus was born in Crete and traveled extensively in the East, where he was universally hailed by the barbarians as a god. Later he returned to Crete to die; and one may still see his tomb, built by his sons the Curetes.[8] Certain scholars see in this story an account of the journeys of Alexander by an irreligious satirist; [9] Plutarch says that Euhemerus with his "false and unfounded mythology, disseminated all kinds of atheism over the world, reducing all deities alike to the names of generals, admirals, and kings pretended to have flourished in old times." [10] And indeed euhemerism has long been a favorite weapon of the skeptical; but also of the religious.

The Christian fathers found euhemerism useful in discrediting the pagan mythology. Augustine tells us in *The City of God* [11] that according to the best knowledge the pagans worshiped deceased men, calling them Jupiter, Hercules, or Pluto. This theory, never completely forgotten (even Boccaccio sometimes used it), attained a vogue in the eighteenth century after it was presented by the Abbé Banier (*La Mythologie et les Fables expliquées par l'Histoire,* 1738).[12] The identification of Banier with euhemerism should not be taken too rigidly, however. He thinks that some myths may be philosophical explanations or allegories and that some, like the myth of Psyche, may be purely aesthetic. Diderot in his *Plan d'une Uni-*

versité advises students of myth to read Banier; and the article on "Fables" in the *Encyclopedia* of Diderot and D'Alembert is a summary of Banier's book. David Hume, as we shall see, was something of a euhemerist. Herbert Spencer's theory that religion originates in ancestor worship is essentially euhemeristic; and Frazer finds some truth in the system of Euhemerus.

3.

The early Church Fathers—particularly the "Africans," such as Tertullian and Cyprian—followed the doctrine of Justin Martyr, which considered the pagan gods to be demons born of the fallen angels and the daughters of men.[13] Whatever was undeniably worthy in the pagan religion and mythology was said to have been plagiarized from Judaism. The idea of plagiarism has sometimes been extended in Christian writings to mean that all pagan religion and mythology was taken from the Jews and corrupted by barbarian plagiarists. The Protestant emphasis on the total depravity of mankind lent a new impulse to this contemptuous view of the pagan world and we find the plagiarism thesis in such seventeenth-century works as G. J. Vossius' *De Theologia gentili, et Physiologia Christiana; sive de Origine idololatriae* (1641), Samuel Bochart's *Geographiae Sacrae* (1646), and Grotius' *De Veritate religionis Christianae* (1639). The Catholic Bishop Huet also advanced this thesis in his *Demonstratio Evangelica* (1679).[14] This theory naturally involved the use of euhemerism; thus Bochart says that Jupiter is none other than Ham, Bacchus is Nimrod, and Saturn is Noah.[15] The plagiarism theory was perpetuated in the eighteenth century by antiquarians and minor mythologists such as Jacob Bryant (*A New System; or an Analysis of Ancient Mythology; wherein an attempt is made . . . to reduce the truth to its original purity,* 1774). A curious tenderness for the claims of the Jews to a special creation remains in Gladstone's *Studies on Homer and the Homeric Age* (1858). The prime minister believed that the pagan myths were degenerate remnants of a primitive revealed wisdom, retained in its pure form by the Jews.

A more fruitful Christian view of myth was the doctrine of Condescension, maintained by Irenaeus and popular in the age of Jerome and Augustine.[16] This doctrine holds that God admitted certain crude and savage elements analogous to pagan cultic practices into Judaism as a necessary step in the revelation of higher truth. This has the advantage of permitting a theory of historical development from the primitive to the civilized and removing some of the stigma from pagan mythology. The historical view was adopted by Eusebius and Augustine. The outstanding seventeenth-century opponent of the plagiarism school (excepting those who were openly skeptical about the infallibility of Scripture, such as Spinoza, Simon, Bayle, and Fontenelle) was the Anglican John Spencer. His book *De legibus Hebraeorum ritualibus* (1686) restated the Condescension theory and was important in making possible the modern literature of comparative religion. Both Robertson Smith and Sir James Frazer insist that Spencer was the founder of "the science of comparative religion." [17]

4.

The Greeks knew something of the Near East, of Babylon, of India, of the "Hyperboreans," of the Ethopians, of Egypt; but their view of the world remained, as Bacon remarks, "suburban." One of the most momentous facts of modern times—for the study of myth as for all of modern thought—has been the new knowledge about foreign lands and primitive peoples. In Bacon's time the literature of foreign travel was already large, and Bacon saw that it offered great possibilities. As he wrote in the *Novum Organum*, it must not "go for nothing that by the distant voyages and travels which have become frequent in our times, many things in nature have been laid open and discovered which may let in new light upon philosophy. And surely it would be disgraceful if, while the regions of the material globe—that is, of the earth, of the sea, and of the stars—have been in our times laid widely open and revealed, the intellectual globe should remain shut up within the narrow limits of old discoveries." In seventeenth- and eighteenth-century Europe it became overwhelmingly clear that across the seas were a multitude of thriving peoples in various stages of development whose "manners" and "fables" [18] could be fruitfully studied. Locke wrote that the philosophers could no longer ignore the "dark entrails of America" [19] and all "those vast, wealthy, and exuberant regions" [20] beyond the seas. It became clear that the history of all peoples would have to be remodeled, for there could be no nation which had not once been primitive. And it became clear that the art, religion, and myth of European peoples showed certain characteristics that were undeniably primitive and must be studied as such. In the following pages I shall try to show how the study of myth has prospered amidst the flood of modern anthropological knowledge.

CHAPTER II

MYTH IN
THE ENLIGHTENMENT

THE FRENCH scholars Salomon Reinach and Lucien Lévy-Bruhl proclaim Fontenelle the founder of the comparative method as a theoretical device in studying mythology and religion.[1] *The Origin of Fables*,[2] Fontenelle's most momentous work, is characteristically a brief *jeu d'esprit*; yet it not only uses the comparative method but it propounds the rationalist-evolutionist study of myth which later eighteenth-century thinkers commonly ignored and which had to await recognition, in England at least, until the late Victorian period, when the English rationalists adopted it. "The followers of Mr. E. B. Tylor," says Andrew Lang in his *Myth, Ritual and Religion*,[3] "do not seem to be aware that they are only repeating the notions of the nephew of Corneille." These notions are, briefly, that myths, whether Greek or American Indian, are survivals of those primitive ages when the mythmaking mind reigned supreme and that only by reconstructing primitive psychology—which we see still at work in something like its pristine form among modern savages—can we understand myth. This idea requires an entirely new conception of what had hitherto been taken as the "history" of ancient times. "If," as Fontenelle says, "one strips one's eyes of convention, one cannot help being appalled to see the whole ancient history of a people, which is only a mass of chimeras, dreams, and absurdities." We must understand, he continues, that fables are the natural product of the primitive mind. Nothing is gained by the common idea that they were simply invented by poets or romancers, or by "the lively imagination of the Orientals." Fables are a necessary cultural phenomenon among all barbarous peoples, whether they are Orientals, Greeks, Jews, Kafirs, Lapps, or Iroquois.

Fontenelle admonishes the reader to reconsider classical antiquity and to realize its long span of time. Cicero himself failed to do this, for has he not, in his *Tusculan Disputations*, demanded a historical impossibility of Homer? Has he not criticized Homer for reading the qualities of men into gods instead of reading the qualities of gods into men? Homer could do only what he did, for Cicero's ethical idea of the gods was entirely unknown in Homer's world. "Primitive men are very brutal," says Fontenelle, "and they rely on force: their gods are nearly as brutal, and only a little stronger; these are the gods of Homer's time." ⁴ The Greeks may be compared with American Indians (the favorite anthropological argument of the Moderns in the seventeenth- and eighteenth-century literary wars between Ancients and Moderns). We shall find astonishing uniformities, says Fontenelle. For example, "the Americans [he means the Peruvians] send the souls of those who have lived sinfully into certain muddy and disagreeable lakes, as the Greeks send theirs to the shores of the rivers Styx and Acheron"—and the sun-god Manco Capac is none other than the Incan Orpheus. Fontenelle insists further upon the fabulous character of Graeco-Roman thought in the twelfth of his *Dialogues of the Dead* (1683), wherein Montezuma, as a spokesman for the New World, argues with Cortez, the apologist for European civilization— "you can't reproach me with one piece of American folly," says Montezuma, "which I will not undertake to match in your countries, and yet I'll engage to bring none into play but Greek follies or Roman." ⁵ And he observes that the Greeks consulted the exhalations of caves for signs of the future and that the Romans invited their gods to eat with them on festival days.⁶

Besides sharply separating myth from history and placing "the fabulous ages" of Greece in the context of other early societies, Fontenelle tries to discover how myths originate. In *The Origin of Fables* he poses the intellectualist explanation which has been adopted again and again from the seventeenth century down to E. B. Tylor and Sir James Frazer. Fables, that is, are said to be primitive science; they are the imperfect result of a conscious search for the causes of observable events. Fables, thinks Fontenelle, are the attempts of "the poor savages" who "explained the effects of nature only by the rudest and most palpable things." "The men who had a little more genius than the others were naturally impelled to search for the cause of what they saw." For example, suppose a savage begins to wonder about the origin of a river: "It is necessary to remember that these ideas, which could be called the systems of those times, were always copied after the best known things. One had often seen water poured from a pitcher; one could very well imagine, then, how a god poured a river out of a pitcher." Fables, we can see—as well as gods—are born of natural facts wrongly explained by "the philosophy of the time." If the gods of the pagans seem to the modern European to be "dominated by the idea of power" at the expense of wisdom and justice, it is because they are survivals of these early times. And if gods were not necessarily very useful to society, they are extremely useful to historians. For precisely because they *are* survivals from primitive times, they "mark all the better the path the imagination has taken in forming them."

Characteristically, Fontenelle sees religion as the refuge of myth. Christianity did not put a stop to primitive superstition, as its apologists have traditionally claimed. "I have never forgotten," he says, "that I was told in my childhood that the elder-tree once bore grapes that tasted as good as wine; but that, the traitor Judas having been hanged from that tree, its fruit had become as bad as it is now. This fable could have arisen only after Christianity." He makes two veiled remarks—in those days of French censorship such remarks had to be veiled—about the Church and its function as a perpetuator of fables. Though fables originate in primitive times, he says, they are nourished in later days by "weakness" and "blind respect for the past." [7]

Fontenelle does not go very deeply into the psychology of the mythopoeic mind, but then he is more interested in a propaganda of Reason against the Church and the Ancients than in folk psychology. He has, however, left us an idea with which to work: the idea, so charmingly expressed in his Cartesian fantasy *The Plurality of Worlds*,[8] of a universal City of Man, a vision of man at home in his universe, of man thinking everywhere in accordance with the stage of his civilization but in accordance, too, with the rationalist temper. It is a hopeful vision; for humanity, thinks Fontenelle, is progressive and myth may someday be entirely outgrown; but the world-wide preponderance of myth—it is still preponderant—is sufficient cause for alarm. Indeed, as he says, "all men resemble each other so much that there is no people whose follies ought not to make us tremble."

2.

Pierre Bayle was an untiring student of mythology. A steady hatred of orthodox Christianity kept aflame his great zeal for discovery. We find in his works the new theory that history must be scientifically factual and that history, properly so called, can deal only with comparatively recent times; [9] we find "the higher criticism" of the Scriptures already in operation; [10] we find an infinite chaos of data on the fables, follies, superstitions, and cruelties of man; and we are invited to consider the weaknesses of our own civilization in the light of the practices of barbarous peoples. "To pass over all the abominations practiced in Peru and Mexico not many years ago, and their prodigious slaughters of men in sacrifice to idols, to which the Spaniards have put a stop in the parts where they have settled; who does not know what shocking superstitions the Indians, the Chinese, and the people of Japan practice to this day; that they fall down to a heifer, to a monkey; that they venture upon burning mountains to consult their demon, bury themselves alive in honor of their false gods, drown themselves out of devotion, which is one of the fairest steps to canonization." [11] To study primitive societies is to study Christianity. "The Christian religion," Bayle writes in his *Dictionary*, "is wounded through the sides of the pagan religion." [12] Rome is still called "a solar city" and the cardinals are clothed in scarlet, like sun-gods.

Bayle's works are full of such observations; yet in all the sardonic prolixity of his writing we find no general theory of myth beyond the assumption that myth is the kind of falsehood which has always satisfied the feeble understanding of mankind and which has been an age-old weapon of oppression in the hands of scheming priests and legislators. Bayle is vague about the origin of myths. The poets seem to be responsible for Greek mythology, or perhaps we must blame the fictitious declamations of the Sophists. There may, indeed, be a general evolution from the age of superstition to the age of reason. As he says in his *Dictionary* article on Briseis, "In Homer's time the ideas of reason were still very much confused." But since he would say the same of Thomas Aquinas' time and of his own time, we are left with no workable notion of historical development.

Bayle's method is not usually theoretical; it is tentative, endlessly curious and exploratory. His article on Adam seems to have been included in the *Dictionary* largely for the purpose of adorning it with long footnotes comparing the Adam myth with pagan myths. In a book by a Father Garasse, who in turn quotes Photius, Bayle finds an Egyptian myth which relates that "Wisdom laid an egg in the Terrestrial Paradise, out of which came our first parents like a couple of chickens." Although Bayle takes pains to refute the allegations of Philo and the Talmudists that Adam was a giant, like Orion or Polyphemus, he is less interested in refuting the allegation that Adam was a giant than in setting down the fact that people have thought he was. The Arabians, he observes, worship a place near Mecca where they believe Adam and Eve, both the size of mountains, first cohabited. Bayle has learned the critical uses of the comparative method. But he does not commonly draw conclusions; he is content to leave his apparently random comparisons to simmer in the mind of the reader.

Bayle's most remarkable essay on ancient mythology is the *Dictionary* article on Adonis.[13] Almost all the people of Greece, he observes, celebrated the rites of this god.[14] He recounts the dark story—the unmanning of the young god by the wild boar, the River Adonis, running red with blood every spring, and the death and resurrection of the god. Theorizing for once, Bayle sees three possible explanations of this myth (in later times Freud, Max Müller, and Frazer, respectively, were to agree with him). First, he believes, this may be a myth of sexual impotence and the resurgence of sexual power; second, it may be a purely solar myth; and, third, it may be a vegetation myth, symbolizing the cycle of vegetative life.

The Syrians, Bayle writes, were even more foolish than the Greeks; for they offered sacrifices to Adonis, they shaved their heads in his honor, their women prostituted themselves to please him on the day of his festival. They mourned and bewailed the passing of Adonis with outlandish cries, but "the mourning ended with joy, for they feigned that Adonis was restored to life." The Emperor Julian, according to Ammianus Marcellinus, was greeted with the howlings of the Adonis worshipers when he entered Antioch in 362 A.D. The cult of Adonis still flourished during Cyril's time. From Alexandria a cask containing a letter was annually dispatched over the Mediter-

ranean to the sorrowing women of Byblus, who, having received it
and learned that Adonis was reborn, ceased weeping and rejoiced.
Lucian reports that he saw the Egyptians throw pasteboard heads of
Adonis into the sea. As later anthropologists have shown, this is an
example of the world-wide practice of agrarian peoples, who throw
images of their vegetation gods into the water to ensure the growth
of the crops.

Besides speculating ingeniously about the Adonis myth, Bayle
makes a tentative gesture toward connecting Adonis with other
ancient gods of similar character. He mentions Plutarch's idea
(*Symposiaca,* Book lv) that Adonis was the same god as Bacchus,
and that the Jews do not eat swine flesh because Adonis was killed
by a boar. He notes that Jerome thought of the "Tammuz" mentioned in Ezek. 8:14, as Adonis. And Bayle correctly believes that
Adonis may be explained in terms of the Egyptian cult of Osiris,
though he does not try to do so.[15]

3.

The transition from Bayle to Voltaire is an easy one. The same
animus inspires them; the same fascinated contempt for the primitive, the mythical, and the religious leads them to make numberless
excursions into the ancient authors and the accounts of modern
voyagers. As we have seen, Bayle could occasionally cease playing
the propagandist and study a primitive myth objectively. So too can
Voltaire, but his value to us (though not to his own time) is severely
damaged by the fact that most of his theories can be taken seriously
only as facets of his polemical purpose.

If we examine his *Dictionnaire Philosophique* and his *Essai sur
les Moeurs* (especially the Introduction, sometimes printed separately
as *The Philosophy of History*), we find a confusing hodgepodge of
opinions about myth and religion. Of course we must expect Voltaire's contempt for myth to get in the way of his understanding
it. Some fables, he says, may be ingenious but none is instructive. The
more ancient they are the more allegorical and incomprehensible.
Fables are "riddles proposed by antiquity to posterity, who understand nothing at all of them." What do we know of Greece before
the Olympiads? He answers that "it is an unknown time, a time lost,

a time of allegories and lies, a time regarded with contempt by the wise and profoundly discussed by blockheads, who like to float in a void, like Epicurus' atoms." We hear much from Voltaire of "ancient charlatans, who judged without reasoning, and who, being themselves deceived, deceived others." Or if self-deceived charlatans are not to be blamed for myth, then we must blame politicians and priests [16] who either invented the myths or adopted them from the mouths of their nurses and made them into weapons of oppression.[17]

If we look for Voltaire's more positive opinions on myth and its origins, we are likely to be further disappointed. He tells us that myth originated in the Orient. "I ask you," he writes to a friend, "if it is not true that the Indian mythology is the origin of all the mythologies of our hemisphere. . . ."[18] Again it is the Persians and Chaldeans who are the source of all rites (and, one presumes, of all myths).[19] But we perceive that this idea arises not only from Voltaire's Oriental studies and his astonishment at the great antiquity of Eastern nations but also from his desire to prove that the Jews abjectly copied all of their mythology and customs from other peoples.

If we look into Voltaire's chapter on Bacchus in the *Essai,* or into his *Dictionnaire* article on Bacchus, where we read that "of all the true or fabulous personages of profane antiquity Bacchus is to us the most important," we find that he is important only because he affords Voltaire an opportunity to besmirch the reputation of Moses by simply inverting the unfounded plagiarism theory of the Christian apologists. The learned Bishop Huet, says Voltaire, points out that, like Moses, Bacchus was saved from the waters where he was adrift in a little chest and that he was instructed in the secrets of the gods. Huet even shows that Moses is the same as Osiris, Typhon, Zoroaster, Aesculapius, Apollo, Amphion, Perseus, Adonis, and Priapus. Christian writers like Huet and Bochart pretend that these demigods were all copied after Moses, but, says Voltaire, the Jewish writings are relatively late and the Moses of Scripture was probably modeled upon the heroes of early and more ingenious peoples.

When he speculates on the mythopoeic psychology, Voltaire arrives at the common opinion of materialists and rationalists from Lucretius down to our own time: that myth and religion originate in terror at the overpowering operations of nature—most specifically, terror at thunder and lightning. On the question of whether or not we should suppose myths to have originally been stories of the wonderful activities of the celestial bodies (modern American anthropologists agree that we should not), Voltaire seems to take both sides; [20] but his argument that in its primitive form myth did *not* concern the sun, moon, and stars—simply that primitive men "did not know enough to embrace so noble an error"—is the more convincing.[21] In his article on "Miracles" in the *Dictionnaire*, Voltaire momentarily approaches an understanding of the psychic qualities of mythmaking—"Miracle," he says, "something admirable; prodigy, implying something astonishing; portentous, bearing with it novelty; monster, something to show on account of its variety. Such are the first ideas that men formed of miracles." If Voltaire had generalized this feeling of power and wonder which he only hints at, he would have come closer than he ever managed to do to a workable understanding of the emotion in which myth begins.

More fruitful than most of his theories was his idea that society was coextensive with man [22]—that "all men live in society," that "we have never seen countries in which they live separate."[23] He gains something too by stressing the social functionalism of religion and myth. Suppose, he says, a villager named Pierre Aoudri wishes to establish himself as the man who is entitled to ring the village bell. His claim to a noble ancestry must be proven. Someone discovers an old iron pot with the initial "A" on it (the initial of the brazer who made the pot). Pierre Aoudri convinces himself that this is the helmet of one of his ancestors. "So," says Voltaire triumphantly, "Caesar descended from a hero and from the goddess Venus." [24] Elsewhere he maintains that the priests of antiquity perpetuated only those traditions which would encourage men, not those which would fill them with cowardice or despair. In so far as these observations suggest a theory that myth is made *ad hoc* to fulfill psychic or social needs, Voltaire agrees with certain modern thinkers—particularly Malinowski. But this is by no means a general theory of Voltaire's: he constantly contradicts it, for example, by repeating the notion that ancient festivals came into being to justify certain myths, instead of supposing that the festivals may have come first—that the myths may be the rationalization or the sanctification of the festivals.

Voltaire made a large collection of mythological lore. But so great is his contempt of myth that he never looks at it closely. His opinions on myth are consistent as propaganda but confused and erroneous as theory.

4.

Voltaire's deism was also, as John Morley says, a polemical attitude rather than a reasoned faith. It is certain that his notion of primitive religion is not very clear—except that, following Locke, he is at great pains to prove that primitive religion is deistic and not polytheistic. His argument, like Locke's, is that whereas "the knowledge of a god is not impressed upon us by the hand of Nature," yet in a state of nature we soon come to know the Deity "from feeling and from . . . natural logic" [25] which God has given us as "He has given feathers to the birds and fur to the bears. . . ." [26] Nevertheless it is hard to imagine a mythology being created by a people who attribute everything to a single impersonal Intelligence; and this difficulty involves Voltaire in a theory of degeneration shared with him by Christian apologists: the theory that most of the known myths, which compose what Voltaire calls "savage mythology," are corruptions of noble but unspecified originals. In the *Essai*, Voltaire furthermore tries to show that there is no proof of the supposed idolatry of the pagan nations. No one, he thinks, ever worshiped a statue or took it for God. Since Voltaire is both materialist and deist, he can see only two possibilities in primitive religion: either one worships a material object or one worships the Supreme Being. This abrupt dichotomy, again, keeps Voltaire from enlightening us on the nature of myth; we shall have to turn to a better philosopher, with whom Voltaire specifically disagrees,[27] for a worth-while hint on this subject.

David Hume's *Natural History of Religion* [28] begins by maintaining that polytheism is the primitive religion of all peoples. There is no "speculative curiosity" or "pure love of truth" among savages such as would lead them to the idea of a Supreme Being: "the ignorant multitude," says Hume, "must first entertain some grovelling and familiar notion of superior powers." [29] From Hesiod's *Works and Days* we learn that in ancient Greece there was not one deity but thirty thousand. Monotheism, says Hume, can only be the invention of people who have attained some philosophy.

The opinion of most American anthropologists is that the argument about monotheism and polytheism is useless as soon as one is said to succeed the other in clear-cut stages of development. The fact that they exist together in the same stage is probably more important than the fact that some stages may be loosely labeled monotheistic or polytheistic. As we shall see later, the belief in monotheism or polytheism has always been partly a matter of temperament. For students of myth, however, Hume's side of the argument has two advantages over Voltaire's. The polytheistic psychology is more productive of myth, and the idea of original polytheism does not entangle us in a theory of degeneration. For in the study of myth the theory of degeneration is surely more misleading than the theory of evolution (though we shall see that Andrew Lang makes effective use of a tentative degeneration theory).

Hume's discussion of the worship of idols was a genuine contribution to the understanding of myth, and it must endear that incomparable philosopher to all students of these matters. Hume's achievement was to see that idols are neither objects contemplated as such nor symbols of the Supreme Intelligence; they are the source and the receptacle of power; they are *used*, not contemplated. They are used to call superhuman powers into effect; they are capable of failure in certain situations, and men even attempt to punish or reanimate them with the power of their own rage. Hume observes that when their prayers are not answered, the Chinese "beat their idols." The animals worshiped in Egypt were said by the Egyptians to be only disguises which the gods once put on to escape the violence of men. After the death of Germanicus, Hume continues, his people "were so enraged at their gods that they stoned them in their temples." When the Tyrians were besieged by Alexander, they put chains on their statue of Hercules to prevent him from deserting to the enemy. Nor do men hesitate to worship a deity who shares the errors of human beings, if by celebrating his power and vitality they think he will be persuaded to help them out of their difficulties. "What conduct can be more criminal or mean," asks Hume, "than that of Jupiter in the Amphitrion? Yet that play, which represented his gallant exploits, was supposed so agreeable to him that it was always acted in Rome by public authority when the state was threatened with pestilence, famine, or any general calamity."

The importance of Hume's observations is that he sees that idol worship and religious ritual are in one sense invocations of power, that power flows back and forth, so to speak, between men and gods, and that primitive religion endeavors to elicit power or sanction from the gods toward the accomplishment of specific tasks, or the avoidance of specific calamities. Men believe in invisible power; also they see sensible objects; an idol, however, is neither merely the one nor the other but a fusion of both. Without this insight of Hume's it would be difficult to understand the mythopoeic mind.

Given this view of mythopoeic psychology, how does Hume account for the gods and heroes of mythology? In the first place, he says, we must see that they are not the products of contemplation; "the vulgar" do not speculate upon the universe. And if they did they would conclude that the universe was created by one god, since "to ascribe any single effect to the combination of several causes, is not surely a natural and obvious supposition." The gods are made out of human passions in operation upon the events of human life. These events are so various, evanescent, and contradictory that the divine powers operating in them must be considered similarly various. Nor are the religious passions of primitive man more extraordinary than the events they apotheosize: "No passions . . . can be supposed to work upon such barbarians but the ordinary affections of human life; the anxious concern for happiness, the dread of future misery, the terror of death, the thirst of revenge, the appetite for food and other necessaries. Agitated by hopes and fears of this nature, especially the latter, men scrutinize, with a trembling curiosity, the course of future causes, and examine the various and contrary events of human life. And in this disordered scene, with eyes still more disordered and astonished, they see the first obscure traces of divinity." Since men live "in perpetual suspense between life and death, health and sickness, plenty and want," it becomes a practical necessity to form some idea of the "unknown causes" of events, not so that events may be explained but *so they may be controlled.* This has been universally done by supposing these causes to be "intelligent voluntary agents" different from men only in being stronger and wiser, or in being sometimes cloaked by the imagination in the out-

ward form of animals or objects. Thus many mythological gods are
doubtless objectified or personified causes. Hume furthermore thinks
that allegory is an early mythopoeic device. There are so many gods,
and their distribution into different departments of life is so particular, that "some allegory" is needed to provide the right god for the
right department.

If deified causes and allegorical beings are characteristic of "mythological religion" (i.e., primitive polytheism), hero worship, Hume
thinks, is even more so. In fact, as he says (following Euhemerus),
"most of the divinities of the ancient world are supposed to have
once been men, and to have been beholden for their *apotheosis* to the
admiration and affection of the people." Hume thought it perfectly
natural that the heavens were filled with "continual recruits" from
the earthly life because the gods of primitive peoples were so little
exalted above men. The emotions of wonder, astonishment, and
affection were sufficient to deify the hero. Accounts of heroes, passing
from generation to generation by word of mouth, were subject to all
the frailties of human memory and to man's habitual love of exaggeration; and mythology is therefore in large part pseudo history.
Hume supposes that Hercules, Theseus, and Bacchus were once real
men whose histories were later mythologized. Euhemerism is certainly
an inadequate system of mythological study; yet it has repeatedly
served the purpose of insisting that mythology is deeply involved in
human emotions and activities. It was a useful corrective to the dogmatic deism of Hume's time.

In Hume's *Natural History of Religion* we have the beginnings
of a pragmatic theory of myth. It is easy to agree with Hume, who
seems to prefer what he calls *"traditional, mythological* religion" to
the *"systematic, scholastic"* kind. The first is more reasonable, since
it does not pretend to be logically consistent. Furthermore, it does
not depend on dogma or rational speculation but on "the present
incidents which strike the imagination"; it is less cruel and fanatical
and is therefore more consistent with the needs of human nature.

5.

Charles de Brosses' *Du Culte des Dieux Fétiches, ou parallèle de
l'ancienne religion de l'Egypt avec la Religion actuelle de Négritie*

(1760) [30] has been admired in later times by E. B. Tylor and Andrew Lang as one of the first books to make systematic use of anthropological knowledge. De Brosses showed, as the title indicates, that the animal and idol worship of the ancient Egyptians was the same as that still existing among the tribes of West Africa and Nubia. He argues that we cannot properly understand mythology until we understand primitive religion and specifically "fetishes," the name given by Portuguese travelers to the idols of the Africans. But to set down his general argument would be to repeat Hume's opinions, which de Brosses admittedly adopts. Nevertheless, he is sometimes more explicit than Hume and he has documented the argument (as Hume did not) with evidence from modern travelers, who have furnished us, as he says, with "essential keys" to mythology.

He begins by observing that the confused classical mythologies have been "for the moderns only an indecipherable chaos." He deplores the tendency to interpret myths as if they were moral or philosophical allegories, or as degenerate imitations of the Old Testament. He thinks that euhemerism is not sufficient. To study the worship of idols, of fetishes, is much more enlightening, he says, provided we do not take them as symbols of god, as both Christians and skeptics have done. We must not be led by the prevailing historical Pyrrhonism, says de Brosses, to deny, because of the obvious absurdity of fetishism, "the certitude of the fact." For in fetishism we have the true psychological foundations of myth; all the ingenious allegorical interpretations of the Osiris myth with its sacred animals will be misleading until we see first of all that these animals are fetishes.

A fetish, he tells us, may be a tree, a mountain, a fish, a lion's tail, a stone, or a plant.[31] An object, animate or inanimate, becomes a fetish when it is taken to be a "powerful preservative against . . . accidents." In a fetish there reside "power," "genius," "manitou" (as far as I know this is the first use by a philosopher of this Algonquin word, which along with the Siouan *wakan*, the Iroquoian *orenda*, and especially the Melanesian *mana*, figures so prominently in twentieth-century writings on myth). Man does not first think of God as a rational Maker, says de Brosses; primitive man imagines only "great power, power of the human kind but endowed with a force entirely superior and limitless, having desires and passions similar to those of men." [32] He is more explicit than Hume about the psychological quality of fetish worship: the savage "united two opposed and simultaneous operations, by attaching invisible power to the visible object, without distinguishing in the crude context of his reasoning the material object from the intelligent power. . . ." De Brosses is saying, in other words, that the mythmaker does not perceive objects as such but as vehicles of efficacious activity analogous to and identifiable with the impersonal powers of the universe projected out of human emotions. Vico and Herder share this opinion with Hume and de Brosses. One feels that had Voltaire devoted himself a little more to theory, he would have been of the same opinion. It is the climactic achievement of the eighteenth century in the study of myth and is an indispensable point of departure for us.

6.

We have already discovered in these writers of the Enlightenment certain useful hints toward an understanding of myth. But skepticism is none the less typical, even of the writers who have given us the hints: they never tire of writing that "fables" are meaningless, absurd, incomprehensible, degrading, frivolous. This characteristic skepticism is well expressed in the article on "Mythology" in the *Encyclopedia* of Diderot and D'Alembert. To be sure, says the *Encyclopedia*, "fable is the patrimony of the arts"; it is useful "to those whose object is to embellish nature and please the imagination." No one can deny that fables have charm—"everything moves, everything breathes in this enchanted world,[33] where intellectual beings have bodies, where material things are animated, where the fields, the forests, the rivers, the elements have their own divinities. . . ." It is an agreeable world but we must not expect to understand it. The article warns against taking Euhemerus and Banier too seriously and maintains that the mythological ages of Greece were rendered completely unintelligible by "the mixture of the inhabitants, the diversity of their origins, their commerce with foreign nations, the ignorance of the people, the fanaticism and barbarism of the priests, the subtlety of the metaphysicians, the caprice of the poets, the mistakes of the etymologists, the hyperbole common among enthusiasts of every kind, the strangeness of the ceremonies, the secrets of the mysteries, the illusion of the magic spells. . . ." In short, says the article, no successful analysis of myth is possible. A thousand errors lie in wait for the inquirer. The methods of study are so imperfect that one can find nothing in mythology but one's own ideal image or a chimerical reflection of the plan of one's own studies. The scientist finds allegories of science; the politician finds political wisdom; the philosopher truth and morality. A complete skepticism will free us from this Circe's island and yet allow us to enjoy myth as the pretty embellishment of art.

Following Locke, the thinkers of the Enlightenment were jealous of that small area of experience they had set aside as the province of Reason. To step out of this province, to take myth seriously, seemed to the philosopher a piece of folly, to the literary critic a serious breach of decorum, and to the moralist a giving of hostages to the priests. This is in my opinion an attractive attitude, even an eminently decent canon of criticism. Yet it will not do; myth has a habit of being sometimes unattractive or indecent. And the cost of refusing to take it seriously is too great. For what was the cost to the Enlightenment of its failure to create an adequately complicated mythology if not the tremendous and destructive intellectual upheavals at the end of the eighteenth century? The terrific forces of the human emotions cannot for long be trifled with. They are not to be controlled and made useful by a too mechanical or indiscriminate repression. (It was no accident, as we suggest in the chapter on psychoanalysis, that the obsessive emotion of the eighteenth century was fear.) But they can be controlled and made useful by the creation of myths. And the first step toward understanding myth is to perceive this truth.

We now turn to two writers whose task it was to lay bare those copious and intricate emotions which are the matrix of mythologies.

Chapter III

TWO PHILOSOPHICAL HISTORIANS

WHILE THE official philosophers of the Enlightenment were busy banishing mythology from serious speculation, the Italian scholar Vico was vigorously affirming its real worth. The *philosophes* were contemptuous of the first ages of man, but Vico unashamedly admired what he supposed to be the rugged and heroic realism of those times. And far from despising myth, he composed a memorable myth of his own about the primitive age. (Joyce has caught the spirit of this myth in the opening pages of *Finnegans Wake*.) Briefly, Vico tells us that after the flood the descendants of Ham and Japhet reverted to savagery; they wandered alone in the vast forests which then covered the earth; they lost their human customs and their language; living close to the fertile mud, they gradually became lusty, grunting giants. There are reports from Patagonia that some of these giants still live, says Vico. Little by little, the earth dried up; exhalations arose, which caused lightning in the heavens. This gave the frightened and awe-struck giants their first idea of religion and started them upon the arduous road to civilization.[1] Out of these first ages came the "exuberant animal" spirit of mythology.[2] Why do Homer's heroes offend neoclassical critics? Why do they shock the civilized reader? Because Homer's heroes retain some of the traits of their gigantic ancestors. There is no impropriety in this: Homer's heroes "are *full of propriety* if one thinks of them in terms of the heroic nature of the *passionate and irritable* men whom he wished to paint." The neoclassical critics, from Scaliger down, have never appreciated "the tableaux of murder which are the sublimity of the *Iliad*," because they have not understood the cycles of Greek history.

In the *Scienza Nuova* (1725) Vico considers everything which the Cartesian mind systematically ignored—nature, society, poetry, mythology, folk psychology.[3] The anthropology of the past he found frivolous and inconsequential. European thinkers—Cartesians not the least—have shown by example how tempting is "the conceit of the learned," the error of imagining primitive man to have the intellectual attainments and preoccupations of European philosophers. The historical mind will have to take a step backward so tremendous that a Cartesian can scarcely conceive of it. How else, Vico asks, "can we recapture the vast imagination of the first men, whose minds, alien to all abstraction, all subtlety, were entirely dulled by the passions, plunged into the senses, and even buried in matter?" If we cannot perform this feat of the imagination, we shall never penetrate the obscurity which has always covered the customs and manners of the earliest nations.

We must use the great principle of comparison, says Vico. We discover that peoples unknown to each other have many "uniform ideas," which are embodied in their fables. Fables must therefore contain "a common motif of truth" by which we can discover the primitive state of society. To study these uniform ideas or "vulgar traditions," to find their causes, to trace their history across the centuries, through all the changes of language and custom—this is the great work of the New Science. Anthropology is a science which does not fail to please God and to offer the most exquisite aesthetic satisfaction to men, a judgment, as we shall see, in which Herder most ardently concurred. "Without doubt," says Vico, "the reader will feel a divine pleasure in this mortal body when he *contemplates in the uniformity of divine ideas this world of nations in all the extent and variety of its places and times.*"

Vico's psychology is somewhat at variance with his theory of the stages of history. For his psychology is evolutionary in the Darwinian sense; but his historical method is not free of the traditional Christian idea of degeneration. The first age was the Age of Gods, during which "theological poets" sang a divine mythological, but apparently nearly inarticulate, language. Then came the Age of Heroes, characterized by the glorious but degenerate and second-rate poems of Homer. The cycle is concluded by the Age of Men, in which language becomes practical and scientific. An important

rule of mythology, as Vico says, is that "the fables imagined by the
first men were severe like their fierce inventors, who had hardly left
their bestial independence [Vico's Age of Gods is of course far from
being tamely ethical; exultant physical power and savagery were
the divine virtues]. Centuries passed, customs changed, and the
fables were altered from their original sense, obscured in the time
of corruption and dissolution which preceded even the existence of
Homer." Homer is not by any means to be taken as a primitive poet
—indeed "Homer" is not *a* poet at all but only a folk name given in
various parts of Greece to bards who sang the heroic songs finally
gathered into the *Iliad* and the *Odyssey*. The Homeric epic has preserved for us the record of the three ages of the world. For though
it represents primarily the Age of Heroes, it retains remnants of the
Divine Age. Furthermore the ritual of Patroclus' funeral, the knowledge of bas-relief, the heroes' contract marriages with outsiders, the
bastard sons who succeed to thrones—all prove that the poems are
relatively late in history. Specifically, they are to be dated at "the
time when the *heroic right* was falling into desuetude in Greece, to
make way for *popular liberty*." [4]

In his *Autobiography* Vico speaks of the "little pleasure he had
found in reading Bacon, who seeks the wisdom of the ancients in the
fictions of the poets." The mythologists, looking for elevating allegories, have not been able to account, as Vico observes in the *Scienza
Nuova,* for the fact that Jupiter committed adultery and that Saturn
ate his children. The *Scienza Nuova* avoids these "terrible perils of
mythology," for it teaches us that unworthy elements have been
added in degenerate times to what was originally true and, if not
gentle, at least worthy of the Age of Gods. This does not mean,
though, that the fables were originally moral or philosophical allegories—and indeed this interpretation is only another example of
"the conceit of the learned" and has filled such books of mythology
as Bacon's and Conti's with absurdity.[5] Despite his Catholicism and
his at least token acceptance of Christian historiography—he says
that his historical principles do not apply to the Jews [6]—Vico does
not agree with Vossius and Huet that pagan myth was copied from
the Jewish religion. Myth is a natural product of all cultures.[7] The
traditional interpretations are only what has been repeatedly got
out of books by scholars who start with preconceived notions. For

his part, Vico resolves to proceed with his researches "as if no books existed."

Following his genetic principle that the New Science must begin wherever its subject began, Vico tells us that primitive thought is pre-eminently poetic—the first men were poets. As Croce points out, Vico makes no distinction between primitive poetry and primitive myth. Vico does not mean that primitive men were all like Dante or Shakespeare; he means that primitive thought performs according to the natural order of things "the most sublime task of poetry;—to animate, to give passion to inanimate objects." Primitive man takes his own thriving imagination as the principle of the universe and he endows everything he sees with his own will and emotions.

As we have seen, Vico supposed that thunder and lightning filled the first men with awe, summoning them out of their promiscuous savagery. From the threatening skies primitive man formed the idea of Jupiter—a god who once belonged not only to the Romans and Greeks but to all pagan nations. He is not, however, an abstract or formalized person: he is the principle of power and life, which resides in the universe. Indeed, as Vico often uses the word "Jupiter" it means the mysterious power indicated by such words as *mana* and *manitou*. "All existence," says Vico, "was in the energy of corporeal forces." The thunder and lightning are the language of Jupiter—they are both visible power and communication, or, in a favorite Viconian phrase, they are "real words."

In the Age of Gods there is no considerable articulate speech. Men talk to each other as Jupiter talks, by signs and gestures and gigantic sounds, "such as we can observe in deaf mutes." [8] This is a crude language, but it is incomparably poetic—a divinely natural fusion of things, energies, and sounds, a tremendous, brutal but beautiful poetry which comes down to historical ages "almost as wide and rapid rivers extend themselves far out into the sea and preserve, in their impetuosity, the natural sweetness of their waters." Civilized language, then, may be supposed to bear traces of its origin. Many abstract words, says Vico, can be traced back to natural objects which were once "real words"; *intellegere* comes from *legere*, "to collect vegetables"; *disserere* means "to scatter seed." [9] Similarly we can trace mythical gods such as Cybele and Neptune, in late times represented with intricate art, to the time when they were simply the earth and the sea and were represented by mute gestures. The myth which became so elaborate and abstract was once only "a sign."

To Vico the neoclassical critics had failed dismally to understand figures of speech and their functions. He thinks it a mistake to suppose them to be artifice or decoration. They are the fundamental language, the only language possible to primitive man. Metaphor, the most brilliant and necessary figure, is "the foundation of language." It is the figure which performs the divine mythological task: the animation of the inanimate. In early times the metaphor meant exactly what it said: it was not, in other words, *thought* to be a metaphor; it was language perfectly fused with reality. Myth is basically metaphorical; indeed, "every metaphor is the abridgement of a fable." Symbols are refinements, abstractions from metaphor, and belong to a more advanced age. We should not imagine that primitive language, any more than primitive myth, is symbolic—an important point on which all competent modern anthropologists agree with Vico.

Having laid down his basic principles for studying the mythopoeic mind, Vico proceeds to outline a modified version of euhemerism in explaining Greek myth. Achilles and Ulysses were actual men, whom the Greeks clothed with fabulous qualities. Vico is something of a crowd psychologist (the theories of crowd psychology can easily be assimilated by euhemerism). He is almost a precursor of Durkheim. In their mythological form, as he says, these Homeric heroes were creatures of the common emotions of an entire nation; they are, as Durkheim and the later French mythologists were to say, "collective representations" of social emotion. Euhemerism, according to Vico, belongs particularly to the Age of Heroes. "The history of early kingdoms," as he says in the *Autobiography,* "was delineated for us by the Greeks in the character of their Theban Hercules. He certainly was the greatest of the Greek heroes and the progenitor of the Heraclids. . . . And since the Egyptians and the Greeks alike observed that every nation had a Hercules (and as for the Latins, Varro enumerated as many as forty), Vico concludes that after the gods the heroes reigned everywhere among the gentile nations." [10] Whether or not Ixion the lover of Juno, and Tantalus, who thirsted among the waters, were real men, the myths concerning them are surely disguised history: for in these myths we see the "pretensions of the plebeians" and the plebeians' war against the patricians.

Euhemerism, however, cannot account for all the mythological beings. Some Greek gods are to be interpreted as social allegories, though they were not at first *thought* of as allegories. Thus Diana, the guardian of fire and water, commemorates and sanctifies the purer life which men led after the establishment of "solemn marriages." Apollo as the "social light which surrounds the heroes born of solemn marriages." After the establishment of family life came the Herculean labor of the Age of Heroes: clearing the forests, subduing nature. The serpents of Hercules, the hydra, the Nemean lion, the tiger of Bacchus, the chimera of Bellerophon, the dragon of Cadmus —these are "so many metaphors which the poverty of language forced the first men to employ to designate *the earth.*" The golden apples of the Greek myth do not represent gold, but ears of wheat; thus we understand that the golden bough of which Virgil speaks represents fertility and growth. And Minerva is the symbol of the civil state which was established after the war between plebeians and patricians.

The similarities between Vico and Hume are clear. Both explain myths by means of euhemerism and social allegory. Both stress the pragmatic relation between man and his gods. Both say that mythological religion is the solicitation of the animate power of the universe, though Vico talks of the creation of myth by poetic metaphor whereas Hume stresses the personification of unknown causes.[11]

Vico's ideas sometimes turn out to be wrong; we shall see as this study progresses that not much is to be gained by picturing primitive man as bestial and completely irrational; that is a prejudice into which Vico's fear of "the conceit of the learned" led him. Yet in an age which was inimical to the study of myth he tried to give to myth what it grievously needed—a firm foundation in the matrix of human emotion and custom. The *Scienza Nuova* is no doubt a cryptic, difficult, and even a quaint book. But Vico's erratic insights give us more valid information about myth than do the *philosophes.*

2.

When, in his *Birth of Tragedy,* Nietzsche wrote about the modern "mythless man" who "hungers after times past and digs and grubs for roots," he was in fact repeating the earlier lament of Johann Gottfried Herder. And when Nietzsche wrote that the tremendous historical scholarship of modern times—this surrounding oneself with cultures alien in time and space—was essentially the search of a frustrated culture for the wild vitality of primitive myth, he might have been commenting upon Herder's life and works. For Herder, the earliest and in some ways the greatest of the German romantics, had expressed before the end of the eighteenth century most of the typical aspirations of German romanticism. His thinking was undeniably fragmentary, and he was often tender-minded and mystical. Yet he was often ingenious and pragmatic, and he was always suggestive. Herder's was the great seminal mind (to use a phrase of which he would approve) of the nineteenth-century romantic movement in Germany.[12]

To be sure, Herder often speaks in the accents of the Enlightenment: he takes comfort in Leibnitzian optimism and believes in the destiny of Science. If we are to have a new mythological art, he says in his *Vom neuern Gebrauch der Mythologie,* we shall have to concern ourselves with two complementary forces: "the reductive and the creative spirits; the analyses of the philosophers and the syntheses of the poets." [13] Yet, as he says, these two spirits seldom work together. And if there has to be a choice between science and myth, Herder will unhesitatingly take myth. The argument is posed in the *Zweites Wäldchen,* where Herder takes issue with C. A. Klotz, the author of a volume called *Epistolae Homericae.* Think how much that was hitherto unknown has been discovered by science, says Klotz; note that new lands have been discovered of late which furnish a multitude of poetic decorations, all far better than Juno, Pluto, Cerberus, and Charon. " 'Discoveries of science!' " cries Herder; "by all means! if they are as widely known, as productive of poetic speech, as rich in imagery, as intuitively clear as mythology; by all means!" But he does not believe that they are: "that the possible gains [from science] can ever equal the innumerable riches of mythological poetry, story, and fable—this I completely deny." [14] Indeed if we are to have science, let it be a "poetic natural science" learned from mythology.

Herder's idea that science might learn from mythology was of course revolutionary in its time. For it meant first of all that the

Enlightenment had made a great mistake in not taking myth seriously.[15] To Herder, Pierre Bayle was a "sprightly busybody" to whom a wrong date in Moreri's *Dictionary* was as important as the idea of God or the origin of Evil.[16] Aside from Herder's intuitive conviction of the importance of myth, his theory of evolution supports the idea that, since myth is a natural creation, it cannot be meaningless: for, as he confidently asserts, "nature never sports without design." Furthermore, on the analogy of biological forms, which were originally chosen once and for all by God and which never disappear, we perceive that myth changes and develops but cannot become extinct, as Voltaire had hoped it would.[17] No doubt there is something of the abnormal in myth—it is similar to dreams and madness. But madness itself is worth our study: In the great *Ideen zur Philosophie der Geschichte der Menschheit* (1783–94) Herder writes, "If the semiotics of the soul should ever be studied in the same manner as those of the body, her proper spiritual nature will be so apparent in all her diseases that the dogmas of the materialists will vanish like mists before the sun." [18] The study of myths (a pastime for blockheads, said Voltaire) may prove wonderfully productive: "a history, a philosophy of the first ages, of the first seed of myth," Herder exclaims in his *Aelteste Urkunde des Menschengeschlechts*—"what a book full of evolution and dynamism! The theology, science, and poetry of the human spirit!" [19]

Before we proceed to Herder's more particular ideas about myth, let us look briefly at his general anthropological method, for it became the typical German method. In his early work, the *Journal meiner Reise im Jahre 1769,* he set down his life ambition: he wanted to write *"ein Werk über das Menschliche Geschlecht! den Menschlichen Geist! die Kultur der Erde! aller Räume! Zeiten! Völker! Kräfte! Mischung! Gestalten! Universalgeschichte der Bildung der Welt!"* [20] Everything that Herder wrote was a partial fulfillment of this ambitious scheme.

In the *Ideen*, Herder tells us that all men are worthy of study: not only Fénelon, as he says, but the New Zealand cannibal, not only Newton but the wretched Pesheray. He is well enough versed in the accounts of voyagers to distinguish nearly a hundred non-European peoples, including thirty-four American Indian societies, and he tries to show how all of these peoples take their widely differing customs and "the tone of their sensations" from their particular environments. His ardent desire, as he says, is to give the world a *Philosophia Anthropologica* to match Linnaeus' *Philosophia Botannica*.

The theoretical justification of the comparative method during the Enlightenment had been the Cartesian doctrine of a universally uniform psychology. The "association of ideas" is *par excellence* the psychology of the comparative method, so that when Locke described the one, he defined the other: "some of our ideas have a natural correspondence and connection with one another; it is the office and excellency of our reason to trace these, and hold them together in that union and correspondence which is founded in their particular beings." [21] Herder, however, was inspired with the nationalism and the time obsession of the romantic historian, and he found the Enlightenment anthropology so superficial as to obscure the differences between people and to rob history of the dimension of time. He needed a compromise with the Enlightenment (for he too wanted to be universal), and it was furnished to him by Leibnitz and the theory of monads. Each monad (Herder would read "each society") is "limited and differentiated," each has its "destiny"; yet each is "representative," each is a "perpetual living mirror of the universe." [22] This compromise between the general and the particular is the theoretical backbone of German anthropology. It allowed Herder to play the citizen of the world, to conceive of a universal study of man, and at the same time to be a patriotic German, forever seeking the divine destiny of his beloved Germany.

Mutability within fixed forms: this is an idea which Herder never forgot. "How many solutions and conversions of one into another do the multifarious species of earths, stones, and crystallizations, and of organization in shells, plants, animals and lastly, in man, presuppose." [23] The variety of species is the plastic art of God; yet even the smallest and most unfinished things are endowed with an imperishable form through which they strive eternally to reach the perfection of which they are capable. Thus each society, like all other organisms, has its unique destiny and those societies—like the Greek —which have most perfectly realized their destinies are the guides and the inspiration of mankind. The guide and the inspiration, but not the model; for no national rebirth of art can come about by copying the ways of other peoples. Posterity will wonder, he says, thinking of the German striving toward Greece, what led us to the terrible delusion of trying to live in an alien age and an alien climate: for this is to fly in the face of nature and history.[24] Homer and Aeschylus could never have written their works in our climate and among our customs.[25]

Like Fontenelle and Bayle, Herder is concerned with the "mythical ages" of Greece, but whereas they sneer, Herder is all admiration. He says in the *Aelteste Urkunde* that the earliest Greek myth, before "the wild voices were silenced" by philosophy, "was *poetic* and *inspired with natural power*." [26] The primitive Greeks represented their gods by a rude stone which later became a herma, or a statue; "the first artists rejected not the most terrible representations." If we are to understand the primitive Greeks, Herder believes, we must compare them with the American Indians and the African savages. The Greek mythmaker spoke to nature as "the rude hunter addresses his dreaded bear, the Negro his sacred fetish." [27] Following Winckelmann and Heyne,[28] he studies Greece as a developing culture which began, like all cultures, in a primitive tribal society. The myths, the sacred groves, the lively superstition of these early agrarian times were the priceless matrix of the most sublime productions of art. The Greek tragedy, he says in *Von Deutscher Art und Kunst*, began in these times in "the impromptu of the dithyramb . . . in the primordial dithyrambic emotion," and later refinements were merely "the husk in which the fruit grew" [29] (a judgment which Nietzsche was one day passionately to reaffirm). Indeed the primitive Dionysian Earth-feeling had imposed upon the tragedy its only essential unities—long before Aristotle.

The influence of Winckelmann on later writers such as Lessing and Herder was of course very great. (Even Spengler's conception of Greek culture is Winckelmannian: "The antique drama," says Spengler, "is a piece of plastic, a group of pathetic scenes conceived as reliefs. . . .") [30] It was Winckelmann who taught the Germans to look on Greek art, as upon Etruscan and Egyptian art, as an organic element of society to be studied in relation to the whole. Winckelmann believed that some Greek statues may be traced back to the fetishes of primitive religion; and he followed the myth in supposing that Daedalus was the original Greek artist and that in him one can already discover the characteristic Greek quality of calm, noble simplicity.[31] Winckelmann, however, is not especially interested in primitive Greek art. He was, as Gilbert Murray observes in his *Five Stages of Greek Religion*,[32] "misled" by Roman and Alexandrian art and mythology. To Winckelmann Greek art was not Dionysian; it was Apollonian: "the universal, dominant characteristic of Greek masterpieces, finally, is *noble simplicity and serene greatness*." [33]

Rather oddly, Winckelmann had taken the statue of Laocoön as an ideal expression of Greek art, and he had, of course, exalted plastic art above poetry. In his *Laocoon*, Lessing sought to repair the damage which he believed Winckelmann had done to critical theory: he felt that tragic and epic poetry must be liberated from the canons of painting and sculpture. Plastic art and poetry, he said, have their own distinct provinces and they must be kept distinct. They are as distinct as space and time, as objects and actions. Virgil and Ariosto made the mistake of giving us "cold descriptions of form"; but Homer never did this: "Homer paints nothing but progressive actions. All bodies, all separate objects, are painted only as they take part in such actions." [34] Homer has established that poetry must concern itself with time and activity.

The effect of Herder's *Erstes Kritisches Wäldchen*, written in criticism of Lessing's *Laocoon*, and the effect of his writings generally, was to suffuse Lessing's rationalism with emotion. Lessing is inclined to think of action as a succession of events—in poetry a succession of symbols. As he says, when Homer wants to give us a picture of an object, such as the bow of Pandarus, he does not do it by objective description, but by recounting the activities which make up the history of the object. But, replies Herder, Homer does not want to give us a *picture* of the bow by telling us its story—he wants to give us a feeling of its vigor, its energy, the strength of its string, the dynamic effects which the bow may have.[35] We may say then that if Lessing adds the dimensions of time and activity to Winckelmann's theory, Herder adds a pragmatic idea of effective power to Lessing's theory. In discussing the bow of Pandarus, as elsewhere in the *Erstes Wäldchen*, Herder grasps that peculiar relation between visible objects and dynamic power which, in the pages on Hume and de Brosses, we said might be helpful in understanding the mythopoeic psychology.[36]

Winckelmann and Lessing had exhorted their countrymen to imitate Greek art. We have seen that Herder considered this a mistake—not because he did not admire the Greeks passionately, but because he was a better anthropologist than Winckelmann or Lessing. He had studied many more people than the Greek and had been struck by their enormous cultural differences. Winckelmann and Lessing were absorbed in the art of Olympian Greece; Herder in the art of primitive Greece. For the student of myth Herder's interest is the more fruitful: the only way to comprehend the myths of an alien people, he thought, was to return to the primitive beginnings where all things become similar. Goethe dramatized this Herderian idea in the second part of *Faust.* How can we effect the marriage of the Faustian and the Classical cultures? How can the modern European mind transfigure itself into a union with the divine mythological Helen? And the answer which Mephistopheles gives to Faust is that he must first descend to the primitive Mothers of all things, in "the uttermost Profound."

But what specific views on myth does Herder offer us? In the first place he contradicts the prevailing eighteenth-century notion that religion begins in fear. It begins in awe and wonder as the simple savage worships Nature, as he contemplates "the great bond of all things." [37] The early mythological religion is a kind of primitive philosophy. In the *Erstes Wäldchen,* however, Herder is concerned to show that mythology is not "a catalogue of universal ideas," not "a masquerade of symbolic and allegorical puppets." [38] The eighteenth-century poets have not understood this and they have consequently misused mythology. They have used it as an end in itself, as a display of learning, or as a mere decoration or illustration to enhance their didactic purpose. To impose "oriental metaphors or mythology" upon our poetry is wearisome and self-defeating. If a poet is to use myth, the myth must be organic with the poem; if it is too consciously sought for, or used merely as a decoration instead of springing out of the necessity of the poem, it is a defect.[39]

Myth is far more fundamental in human culture than has been

thought in the past, says Herder. The first men spoke a poetic language, the very language of mythology. "The hypothesis . . . that speech was a direct gift of the Deity is contrary to all analogy, and destroys the wonderful unity of Nature; for everything grows or develops, and nothing is made perfect at once. Language has grown like a tree from some small seed, and man is the author of his own speech. In the childhood of man, whilst men were still half beasts, soon after, according to the fables, men and beasts ceased to understand each other, speech was a song or poetry full of pictures and images." [40] Myth is the folk spirit speaking—"even in its wildest lines and worst conceived features," he says in the *Ideen,* "it is a philosophical attempt of the human mind, which dreams ere it awakes, and willingly retains its infant state." [41] The greatest poets—Homer, Dante, Shakespeare—were mythological poets; through them the primitive spirit of their own nations spoke. They are akin to the bards and ballad singers; in his anthology called *Volkslieder,* Herder places the songs of Shakespeare side by side with the songs of the Lapps, the Greenlanders, and the Peruvians.

The characteristic and governing conception of Herder's philosophy of myth (as we hinted above in the discussion of the bow of Pandarus) is the idea of eternal developmental force. The conception is well stated in his *Conversations on God;* as Frederick Burkhardt writes in the Introduction to his translation of this work: "The two great themes of the 'Conversations' are the interrelated conceptions of divine immanence and the dynamism of nature. God is found revealed in every point of nature. The universe is conceived as a unified complex of forces, arranged in a hierarchy, and operating according to immutable laws, which are at one and the same time the evidence of the divine power, and the activity of God himself realized in the world-order. The whole is continuous; there are neither gaps nor leaps in nature. Quiescence is negation; death is merely apparent."

"All things are full of organically operating omnipotence," Herder writes in the *Ideen.*[42] Myth is the poetic embodiment of vegetative growth (*Wachstum*), of operating efficacy (*Wirkung*). "The whole Egyptian mythology rests not in forms and shapes," he exclaims characteristically in the *Aelteste Urkunde,* "but in powers and symbols: the highest power of nature is *fruition,* population . . . the whole Egyptian mythology bespeaks . . . the blessing of Earth, the Nile, the animals, men—thereof speaks everything! Onions and Garlic! [43] Mendes and Apis! Man and Woman! Generative vitality was the theme of their mythology, interpreting all. . . ." [44]

Myth is a rhapsodic affirmation of life. And since, like all organisms, a national mythology is plastic and changing, we cannot simply "receive" a mythology from an earlier people. What Winckelmann and Lessing ask us to imitate is nothing more than the lifeless forms and pictures precipitated at a late period of Greek culture: seen *in toto* Greek myth was a process and not a static pantheon of Olympian gods.

These nearly mystical insights are indispensable to the loosening up of our common intellectualist prejudices; and without this useful spadework of Herder (and Vico!) we could scarcely develop a pragmatic view of myth. "Organically operating omnipotence," however, is a somewhat intangible thing, and, as we might expect, Herder is correspondingly vague about the various mythological guises it may assume. As an ardent patriot, he finds euhemerism plausible; it allowed the Greeks, he observed in *Von neuern Gebrauch der Mythologie,* to exalt "a stout farmer boy" into a Hercules and to make the Argonauts and the conquerors of Troy into demigods. "What is Scamander and Olympus and all the sacred places and stories which were the original stuff of . . . mythologies?" he asks in a poetically euhemeristic mood. "I see them in accounts of voyages, I extract their poetical beauties from ancient history; what are they? Heavens! I have all this in my own land, in my own history; around me lies the material for this poetical achievement. But one thing is lacking: Poetic Spirit." As a philosopher and moralist, he finds it useful to think of myth as "allegory! personified nature, or disguised wisdom!" Greek myth "leads Philosophy to earth in order to show her in action." [45] Mythology has been treated as a poetical picture gallery, as a chemical laboratory, as history, as the physical science of antiquity, as poetry, according to the character of him who treats it. This is precisely the complaint against the interpretation of myth made by the *Encyclopedia;* but with Herder it is not so much a complaint as a recognition that a philosophy of myth must be hospitable to various and even contradictory explanations—that what a myth *is* depends partly on what it is used for and on who is interpreting it.

Of myth as philosophy Herder has this to say in his *Ueber Bild, Dichtung, und Fabel:* myth is "the personification of effective powers"; it expresses the clashes and harmonies of emotional forces. "The oldest mythology and poetry, therefore, is a *philosophy of natural law;* an attempt to explain the evolution, the enduring, and the annihilations of the universe. Thus it is to the stupidest Negro and the cleverest Greek; further cannot, may not, and will not the human spirit meditate." [46]

In a more objective mood Herder, following C. G. Heyne, divides the province of Greek mythology into three parts: "The mythology of the Greeks flowed from the fables of various countries: and these consisted either of the popular faith, the traditionary accounts that the different generations preserved of their ancestors, or the first attempts of reflecting minds to explain the wonders of the earth and give a consistency to society." Here we have for the first time the divisions of mythology which later students found it useful to make: (1) the folk tale and folklore (if we may take "popular faith" in this sense); (2) the legend, a partly euhemeristic story of historical pretensions; (3) the myth proper, an explanation or dramatization of nature or society. Cosmogonic myths, says Herder, are later in the evolutionary scale than "the harsh primitive legends," the latter being amalgamated into the former, when "human heroes and patriarchs were sung and placed by the side of the gods." [47] But this salutary scheme of Heyne and Herder was to be long neglected by mythologists who, like Herder, himself, were concerned with nature worship and the philosophy of nature, and who were consequently but too eager to see philosophy and science in myth.

Herder has all the qualities which we may justly deplore in German (indeed, in European) romanticism. His thought is fragmentary, his works mostly unfinished and chaotic; he is humorless, prolix, exclamatory, and despite his great intelligence, he sometimes shows that egregious crudeness of sensibility which so often accompanies sentimentality and power worship. Sometimes in the Herderian forest of capital letters and exclamation marks, one longs to turn back to Fontenelle or Voltaire. Yet the journey is eminently worth making: we cannot help admiring Herder's boundless ingenuity, his energetic curiosity, his rich sincerity. And his romantic temperament takes myth as seriously as we know it must be taken.

Hume, Vico, and Herder all stress the pragmatic and above all the deeply *human* origin and purpose of myth. But especially in Herder we begin to find the influence of nature worship and of natural science. The nineteenth century almost uniformly treated myth either as natural philosophy or as nature poetry; and in a sense the nineteenth-century theories must be regarded as a long detour to be traversed before we can get back to the main road. Nevertheless, the philologists and ethnologists of the nineteenth century have much to tell us.

CHAPTER IV

MYTH, HISTORY, AND PHILOLOGY

*I*N OUR day it requires an effort to recapture and understand the eighteenth- and nineteenth-century passion for philology. In his youthful and buoyant book *The Future of Science* (written in 1848) Ernest Renan acclaimed philology as the great intellectual discipline of modern times; to Renan philology was historical criticism on the grand scale as the Germans conceived it; it was the science of humanity, the science of the human mind. It was the rigorous examination of texts by a man who—besides being a textual critic—was a historian, an anthropologist, a linguist, and an artist.

The founders of the august German "science" of philology were K. F. Hermann, C. G. Heyne, and J. A. Wolf. These scholars, says the Belgian philologist K. Hillebrand, and with some reason, effected "the deliverance of Greece." [1] Wolf, the greatest textual scholar of the three, thought that philology was nothing less than "the science of antiquity," which could restore the ancient world in its organic totality so that we could understand it "in every possible sense." [2] Doubtless philology cannot do what Wolf said it could do. For, compared with broader, anthropological and historical methods, philology is a narrow method indeed, and it cannot help conditioning its discoveries accordingly. But philology, directed by historical and anthropological knowledge, can do what Wolf's *Prolegomena to Homer* (1795) did: reconstruct in the context of social and religious history the biography of a body of literature from the early folk tradition down to the last scholiast. Wolf's great feat was the classification of the sources of our knowledge about Homer and antiquity in general. Wolf is suspicious of traditional interpreta-

tions of myth. Myths about Homer, for example the myth which
portrays Cadmus as the inventor of writing, had hitherto obscured
the study of Homer. Thinking, perhaps, of Herder, he felt that,
though comparative mythology was obviously useful, there had
been too much generalized speculation about savagery and myth
and that it was time to get down to grammatical, textual, and historical problems.[3] In his *Darstellung der Alterthumswissenschaft*
(1807) he wrote: "We have hitherto sought the materials [of myth]
in the easier ways, but they are hidden in so many remote places that
bringing them together is one of the most arduous of tasks." [4]

The post-Wolfian philologists set themselves to this task with a
truly Teutonic zeal, and they produced works of scholarship then
unprecedented in their scrupulousness of inquiry. We shall look but
briefly into these ponderous and tedious authors, and then pass on
to Otfried Müller, a philologist who is still of positive use to us,
and to Max Müller, whose mistakes are still given considerable cur-
rency by some contemporary writers.

2.

The German romantics were as a rule enthusiastic searchers after
myth. Hegel spoke for many of his countrymen when he longed
for a "polytheism of art" and imagination, a plastic and mythological
philosophy.[5] The search for myth as the key to national artistic
and religious salvation, so ardently carried on by the poets, critics,
and philosophers, had its effect on philology. Friederich Creuzer—
along with G. Kanne, J. Gorres, and Friedrich Schlegel—studied
Oriental mythology as well as the Greek. In his ponderous work
called *Symbolik und Mythologie der alten Völker, besonders der
Griechen* (1810 ff.), Creuzer maintained that primitive Greek
mythology was a kind of occult symbolic representation of the
spirit of the universe. The symbolism had two sources: the stupidity
of the people, who could apprehend the hidden universal spirit only
by means of the symbols which revealed it and the benevolent priests,
who had learned a recondite symbolism from the Orient and who
used this knowledge to instruct the people. The Greek mythology,
as we know it, is only a faded version of this primitive symbolic
philosophy, though, as Creuzer thought, the Dionysus and De-

meter myths preserve it in a more primitive form than the myths
of the Olympic gods. Thus the mythologist needs a knowledge of
the East and a talent for divination if he is to understand Greek
myth.[6]

In answer to Creuzer, J. H. Voss renewed the skeptical attitude of
the Enlightenment, claiming that the inventions of scheming priest-
craft had cast a great shadow over Greek myth.[7] In a series of letters
to Creuzer, Hermann maintained that primitive Greek myth is
neither symbolic nor allegorical; it is poetic cosmogony whose only
genuine characteristic is personification. As he says, "all that one
needs to understand [myth] is the names and epithets of the gods
and their etymological interpretation." [8] This is a doctrine which
will concern us later.

3.

The "science of antiquity" which Wolf had hoped for, could
scarcely be said to have emerged. The utmost confusion prevailed
among the post-Wolfian students of myth—I have not mentioned
Buttman, Lobeck, and Welcker—during the first two decades of
the nineteenth century. A philologist who combined the religious
sensitivity of Creuzer, the rationalism of Voss and Hermann, and
the historical rigor of Wolf was grievously needed; he appeared
in the person of Otfried Müller. Müller was not in a strict sense a
"scientist of antiquity," but he was the most levelheaded and at the
same time the most perceptive of German philologists.

In his *Introduction to a Scientific System of Mythology* [9] Müller
achieved some striking results by judiciously combining a fine
intuitive sense with a strictly limited field of research and careful
historical reconstruction. He considers Greece, and Greece alone—
ignoring Sanscrit and the Indian mythology, which by 1825 were
well known in Germany. In the traditional German manner his
method is formal and genetic—three of the chapters are called
"External Idea of the Myth," "Internal Idea of the Myth," "Sources
or Origin of the Myth." He is dogmatic about his historical method,
the "real nature" of a myth cannot be found except historically.
We must know the Greek language and the geography, history, religion, and civil society of Greece. On the other hand, the only way
to learn about primitive Greece is to decipher the myths it has left

to us. This partial contradiction arises from another of the limits Müller places on his study—he decides not to try to understand the history of prehistoric Greece by means of comparative anthropology, though he is of course aware of that method and briefly pays his respects to the American Indian adoring "his Great Spirit at the murmuring stream," the ecstatic dance of African ritual, "sounds of religious wisdom from India" (here he is sarcastic), the orgiastic worship of Baal, the nature worship of Egypt.

He realizes from the Wolfian manner of studying the Greeks that Greek myth as we know it has undergone countless changes at the hands of bards, priests, poets, anthologists, interpolators, and scholiasts. This being so, the method of analysis is obvious: the myth must be subjected "to a treatment the converse of that which it received from the ancients"; as he says in effect, we must go back down the very complicated stairway which the myth has ascended if we are to find where it came from and consequently what it is. Müller realizes that this cannot be done without some outside referents: it is not just a matter of juggling texts. Thus his method is to trace specific myths back to a specific event which both myth and history record—an invasion, a migration, the building of a city, the establishment of a colony or, especially with the earliest myths, a religious worship. Müller exempts cosmogonic myths from this generalization but says that among the Greeks these are only one tenth of the whole. He does not dogmatize about the psychology which attached myths to events. He feels, to be sure, a kind of Herderian joy when he considers the early Greeks: he speaks of "the noble simplicity of those ages" and asks, "must not . . . even the first dawning of the glorious and beautiful give indications of its native character?" He does not agree with those who think that primitive men are stupid human brutes. We should not, as he rightly says, exclude any idea from primitive mentality without positive proof that it does not belong there. Furthermore there is no evidence of any ancient Greek caste of knavish priests (as Voss had thought) or of sublime teachers (as Creuzer had thought).

What the learned men of Greece called myths, Müller observes, consists of a mass of "*narrations in which the deeds and destinies of individual personages are recorded and which all relate, by the way they are connected and interwoven, to a period antecedent to the historical era of Greece and separated from it by a tolerably distinct boundary.*" This Müller takes to be the correct "external idea of the myth." The Greeks distinguished carefully between the mythical and historical periods of their native land. And, says Müller, narratives which describe specific and actual events are myths only because they blend these events into the more magnificent events of the mythical age. As we shall see, this insight applies not only to Greek myth but to the myth of many other peoples, though not quite in the manner which Müller supposes.

If we are to grasp the "internal idea of the myth," says Müller, we shall have to think of a myth as composed of two elements: the actual and the imaginary, the real and the ideal. In the myth of Demeter, we find that to the historical fact of Demeter worship at Eleusis has been joined the imaginary account of Demeter's coming among the Eleusinians as a maid and instructing them in their mysteries. The Arcadian myth of Callisto expresses other fusions of the real and the ideal. This myth tells us that Callisto, the companion of Artemis, was seduced by Zeus and turned by the wrath of Artemis into a bear. This imaginary story can be traced to a religious cult of Artemis in which the goddess was waited upon by virgins called "she-bears." The word Callisto, furthermore, seems to be a name or title of honor belonging to Artemis herself. Now since the mythical Callisto is also a bear, she "is just nothing else than the goddess and her sacred animal comprehended into one." In other words the primitive agrarian Greek held both Artemis and the bear sacred as sources of vigor and fertility; and he composed the myth of Callisto, which unites these imaginary and real objects of worship. The later version of the myth tells us that Zeus rather than Artemis transformed Callisto into a bear; but this, thinks Müller, was an attempt by the poets to dissociate Artemis both from the debauched Callisto and from the bear, since in later times Artemis had a very high reputation for chastity, which the poets could not without indelicacy besmirch.

Most myths, Müller tells us, refer to a definite existing phenomenon "and were formed expressly for it." "One myth relates to some old usage, another to an ancient regulation of public life, a third to the festival of a god, and its usual attendant representations." Those who find the cause of a custom or a rite in mythology are using just the reverse of the correct method. But *why* are myths formed expressly in relation to definite phenomena? Here Müller is only partly enlightening. His explanation is that myths are etiological—"They all aim at accounting for the origin of these things still existing. The mythology of the Greeks everywhere exhibits traces of this *striving at explanation.*" It is the imperfect rationalist attitude toward myth which we shall meet again in our discussion of Tylor and Lang. If Müller had seen that myths fuse "the real and the ideal" not for the purpose of explaining "the real" (i.e., the objective fact) but for the purpose of transmuting "the real" into a magical reality, he would have been nearer the mark. But this is to anticipate.

Having said that we should not deny the primitive mind any kind of thought without good reason, that myths unite "the real and the ideal," and that they are made for specific purposes—thereby providing us with an incipient definition of myth—Müller puts the whole into a historical strait jacket. He falls victim to the traditional fallacy of thinking that there was a time when no one could distinguish the real from the ideal, when myth was "the current expression of civilization," and that as soon as the difference between the real and the ideal became apparent, mythopoeic activity vanished. Müller even dates the disappearance of Greek mythmaking and the ascendency of philosophy and history at the sixtieth Olympiad. Half of the romantic melancholy over the primitive Golden Age which had vanished forever—as well as half the artificial historical anthropology of the nineteenth century—might have been avoided by the reflection that so far as we know man's mind has been capable of both fusing and distinguishing between the real and the ideal *in all ages.* But, though Müller's general historical theory is misleading, his specific reconstructions of history and myth—which link his name with Niebuhr—remain of unquestionable value. He thinks of myth as being close to the identifiable facts of human life and so escapes the excessive fancies of most other nineteenth-century writers on our subject.

Otfried Müller is the best of the mythologists who have limited themselves to the nonanthropological method. The purely literary-historical method has the advantages of its limitations—it does not have to indulge in questionable comparisons of primitive Greeks with Hurons and Ashantees, Aryans and Eskimos; it leaves ample room for the critic's common sense, taste, and intuition. On the other hand, eschewing anthropological referents can lead to a kind of critical inbreeding which stifles and obscures what it seeks to illuminate. Müller's adoration of the Greeks was inspiring. Yet the Greeks limited his critical sense. Perhaps nothing could give us a clearer insight into his devotion to the remains of Greek antiquity than his remark that if the Greek writers have left us an authentic interpretation of myth, *we cannot yet recognize it*. The heart's desire of every philologist is that someday his texts will reveal the Truth.[10]

4.

While Otfried Müller was carrying on his exclusively Greek researches, other scholars, such as Bopp, Pott, Burnouf, and Friedrich Schlegel, were elaborating a comparative philology which was to entangle Greek myth inextricably with Sanscrit, the Vedas and the "Aryas." The most famous of the later mythologists who committed themselves to the new Oriental discoveries were Adalbert Kuhn in Germany (*Die Herabkunft des Feuers und des Göttertranks,* 1859), Michel Bréal in France (*Hercule et Cacus, étude de mythologie comparée,* 1863), and in England Max Müller. Renan, who in his *Future of Science* (1848) had hailed the universally wise philologist and condemned the pedantic "logophile," wrote twenty-odd years later that the Sanscrit scholars had effected "a completely decisive revolution" in the study of myth and that mythology had been proved to be no more than a vast play on words, most of which could be shown etymologically to have something to do with the sun.[11] "Another magnificent sunset looms in the myth of the death of Heracles," sighed Max Müller poetically, and Bréal maintained in his *Mythe d'Oedipe* that Oedipus was the sun battling the storm clouds represented by the Sphinx. Later in "The Great Gladstone Myth" Andrew Lang was to show, with suitable etymologies, that Mr. Gladstone himself was a sun-god.

Max Müller was the most influential of these etymological nature-mythologists, and from 1860 to about 1880 his theories were triumphant both in England and on the Continent. He had studied under Bopp in Berlin and Burnouf in Paris; in England, where he lived for most of his life, he combined a vast store of philological learning with a temperament perfectly characteristic of all that was second-rate in Victorian aesthetics and morality.

Max Müller's theory of myth is based upon the well-known "Aryan" linguistic hypothesis, according to which Sanscrit, Greek, Latin, Gothic, Slavonic, Celtic, and other languages are all descended from a common original, which may be deduced by comparing similar words in the known languages. It is important to note, however, that *in practice* Max Müller usually takes Sanscrit to be the original tongue and the Vedas to be the authentic scripture of the original Aryan people. In the early statement of his theory, the essay called "Comparative Mythology," [12] Max Müller maintained that he could discover the character of the Aryas by means of etymology. I do not intend here or elsewhere to dispute Max Müller on technical questions of philology.[13] But since Aryan is a language no one can possibly know and since a known language is only of limited utility in studying the ways of the people who speak it, philological reflections upon the ways of the Aryas cannot carry much weight. This judgment is reinforced when we discover that Aryan thought is remarkably like the more sentimental, nature-worshiping side of Victorian thought. These primitive men, as Max Müller tells us in "Comparative Mythology," were "noble and pure"; they were not savages but "ancient poets of language"; nay, they had "the healthy and strong feelings of a youthful race of men, free to follow the call of their hearts—unfettered by the rules and prejudices of a refined society and controlled only by those laws which Nature and the Graces have engraved on every human heart."

The power of language is, to Max Müller, absolute; all other human accomplishments and activities somehow proceed from it or are governed by it; it is an autonomous power. The Vedas show us how the human mind in its early stages "is driven necessarily and inevitably by the irresistible force of language." (In a remarkable passage Max Müller shows that the rite of suttee and the deaths of thousands of Hindu women who have committed suicide in this rite can be attributed to a mistake in the translation of a received text.) The Aryan language was made up entirely of what we now call "roots," which were words expressing action.[14] These words all partook of "the fundamental metaphor," i.e., the primitive act of projecting human will and vitality into the external operations of nature: [15] "the creation of every word was originally a poem, embodying a bold metaphor or a bright conception." [16] There is of course a basic truth in this. We did not object when we found similar theories in Vico and Herder. It is a matter of what one thinks poetry is. To Vico this primitive mythopoeic activity was rough and substantial; in Herder it was firmly grounded in nature; in both Vico and Herder it was a serious activity deeply involved in the psychic and moral foundations of the human personality. But to Max Müller this mythopoeic mind dwelt upon the dreamy Sun kissing the Dawn who "trembled and grew pale." This is the language of Swinburne and Morris at second best—not the language of primitive man.

The Aryan language was crippled by the limits of its expression, for it was capable of *nothing but* poetic metaphor, mostly describing natural phenomena. The Aryas could not say "the sun rises"; they had to say "Night gives birth to a brilliant child." Similarly, "in the ancient poetical and proverbial language of Elis, people said, 'Selene loves and watches Endymion,' instead of 'it is getting late.' " This curious linguistic difficulty—at once poverty and abundance— is responsible for mythology, which Max Müller describes as a "disease of language." [17] He means by this that myth is a kind of insanity to which men were vulnerable because their insufficient language was incommensurable with the emotional demands placed upon it. And indeed, so Max Müller feels, no one but a madman could imagine the outrageous story of Kronos swallowing his children or of Deucalion and Pyrrha throwing stones behind them and thus begetting the human race; nor could any healthy mind imagine the Gorgon, the chimera, or the other creatures of this period of seemingly "inexplicable monstrosities."

Now Max Müller's theory, which purports to account for myth and all its enigmatic characteristics, is very simple. We are told that when the Aryas dispersed and migrated into Europe, the meanings of the original metaphors were forgotten, though the metaphors themselves remained in the separate dialects. Myths, then, are stories told to explain or justify figures of speech no longer understood.[18] For example, there were several Aryan synonyms meaning sunset; in Greece the meanings of most of these words were forgotten. One of these meaningless synonyms can be discovered in the word "Endymion." "Endymion" was said to have gone to the place of Night where "Selene" discovered him asleep and fell in love with him. To an Aryan this might mean that the sun had set and that he had met the moon. But it meant nothing to the Greeks, who, in order to explain it, told a story about a prince of Elis whose name happened to be Endymion. Thus it was said that this prince fell asleep on Mount Latmos (derived from the same root as "night") and was loved by a maid called Selene.[19] Two operations, then, are involved in the creation of myth: (1) the misunderstanding of a poetic metaphor expressing an idea about the sun or moon, and (2) ascribing the activities which the meaningless metaphor seems to recount to mundane agents in order to explain it. The first operation is a verbal mistake, a pun—for example on the word Endymion—exactly the process by which Joyce makes so much personal mythology in *Finnegans Wake*. The second operation is a kind of secularizing of divine wisdom; that is, it is philosophy or science.

Now although "the disease of language" theory purports to account for the more savage elements in Greek myth, Max Müller in fact sheds no light on them. For example, the myth of Apollo and Daphne means to him something like "the opener of the gates of the sky" (the sun) pursues "the burning one" (the dawn). Daphne turned into a plant of the same name (the laurel) to escape Apollo. Andrew Lang responds to this idea by pointing out that Daphne ought to be seen as a goddess created to explain or sanctify the use of the laurel plant in primitive ritual.[20] In Max Müller's discussion of Artemis and Callisto (to whom we have referred in the paragraphs on Otfried Müller) he is more interested in identifying Callisto with the Bear constellation than with a possible totemistic bear cult, as Andrew Lang thinks he should have done.[21] Max Müller is as determined as Bulfinch to bowdlerize mythology.

That this theory of mythology—even if it could be accepted as a theory at all—is limited was admitted by Max Müller himself, especially in his late work called *Contributions to the Science of Mythology*. It cannot enlighten us, he says, about ancestral gods nor about such "abstract deities" as Psyche, Eros, Themis, and Moira. It confines itself in theory to "Aryan" mythologies and in practice to the Hindu and Greek—largely ignoring the primitive peoples of the world.

The theory has three other major limitations. (1) It is essentially a theory of degeneration—it is modeled on the traditional Christian historiography whose remnants we found in Vico, except that the chosen race is the Hindu and not the Jewish. The primitive Golden Age, as Max Müller thinks, was followed by a period of corruption and ignorance; this was followed by our period of "withered thought," which to Max Müller is another way of saying our period of *withered words*.[22] Nothing is more revealing of Max Müller's inadequate psychólogy than his idea that words, once poetic metaphors, are now "mere names"; [23] whereas words are now as always effective instruments of human emotions capable of mythopoeic activity. (2) The basic methodological objection to Max Müller's theory is, of course, that he sees nothing but language—language above time and place, above history and anthropology. Etymologies can indeed play an important role in the study of myth; it is useful to know that *Zeus-pater* and Jupiter are cognate with the Sanscrit *Dyaush-pitar,* but even these highest of all the gods were born in, or re-created in, entirely distinct cultural and geographical environments—processes which philology is powerless to study. (3) Max Müller was interested mainly in the "first stage" of myth, when myth was "a poetical and philosophical conception of nature," and very little in the "second stage," when myth "excludes nothing that can touch the hearts of men." [24] Now since it is entirely possible that no such first stage ever existed and since the study of myth asks little more than the question, "What *is* the relation between myth and the hearts of men?" it is hard to believe that Max Müller contributed anything very considerable to the "science of mythology."

Clearly, the idea that philology should be "the science of antiquity," that it was nothing less than the historical criticism conducted by a man versed in anthropology and art, belongs to an earlier age—the heroic age of German scholarship, which was born with Heyne and Wolf and declined in the 1830's with the death of Otfried Müller. During the brief ascendancy of Max Müller, the philological method was dealt a nearly mortal blow by the ethnologists. To these we now turn.

CHAPTER V

THE ENGLISH RATIONALISTS

AFTER THE French Revolution there was a curious lapse
of interest, among the mythologists, in primitive races. The center
of anthropological and mythological studies shifted from France
to Germany. The Higher Criticism, which dealt with relatively
civilized peoples like the Jews, the Hindus, and the Greeks, absorbed
the interest of the scholars. The regal sky and sun-gods which the
philologists posited were not spiritually at odds with the reactionary
peace which had been imposed on Europe. (Max Müller chides
Andrew Lang for "having recourse to savages.") The discovery of
a new "primitive" center of civilization in India provided a sub-
stitute for the discredited conservative idea that the Jews were the
fathers of mankind and appeared to lend new credence to the old
idea of degeneration, never successfully exorcized from nostalgic
minds.

The combination of liberalism and rationalism which a broad
and inclusive cultural anthropology seems to require appeared in
England after 1860, and England became the center of anthropological research. The theory of Darwin had apparently laid the ghost
of degeneration and made the study of the lower orders of life
imperative; the democratic politics of the Victorian savants kept
the study of savages from seeming distasteful or degrading; the
prevailing rationalism made possible a newly attempted speculative
synthesis of the history of mankind—a synthesis which (though in
many ways misleading) brought a new note of sanity into the study
of myth before that synthesis was partially discredited by the
sociology of the Frenchman Durkheim, the antievolutionary pragmatism of the American anthropologists, and the psychoanalysis
of Freud.

49

2.

E. B. Tylor, the peer of Thomas Huxley, John Morley, and Leslie Stephen, was the official Victorian ethnologist. His book called *Primitive Culture* was published in 1871; it is still esteemed by most American anthropologists. Tylor's theory is that the culture of mankind is subject to the same process of evolution as is animal life in general, that cultures in all parts of the world (barring the occasional direct influence of culture upon culture) develop uniformly through the same stages of civilization and that this general law holds even for the most spiritual of man's inventions. It is easy to oversimplify Tylor's thought, however, and the above description of his theory should be taken to apply only superficially to a mind which was first of all judicious and objective and, only then, theoretical.

Like a great many other Englishmen of the nineteenth century, Tylor got his first ideas of mythology from Lemprière's *Classical Dictionary*, that confusing compendium of allegories, euhemerisms, and etymologies.[1] But by 1871 Tylor had come to reject the allegorical interpretation except for very limited kinds of myth, such as the Hesiodic story of Pandora and the medieval beast fables. Euhemerism he finds relatively useless and linguistic interpretations dangerous. He attributes the confusion which he finds in most mythologists to their ignorance of those modern savage peoples among whom the competent observer may still see myth in the actual process of creation and use. To the comparative anthropologist, he says, "Baiame the creator, whose voice the rude Australians hear in the rolling thunder, will sit throned by the side of Olympian Zeus himself. Starting with the bold rough nature myths into which the savage moulds the lessons he has learned from his childlike contemplation of the universe, [the anthropologist] can follow these rude fictions up into times when they were shaped and incorporated into complex mythologic systems, gracefully artistic in Greece, stiff and monstrous in Mexico, swelled into bombastic exaggeration in Buddhist Asia. He can watch how the mythology of classic Europe, once so true to nature and so quick with her ceaseless life, fell among the commentators to be plastered with allegory or euhemerized into dull sham history."

Despite his resolve to get back to "ceaseless life" Tylor has the intellectualist prejudice of the eighteenth-century philosophers. On the surface at least, he is a veritable Fontenelle; he tells us that myths must be studied in the context of "primitive philosophy" and that "man's craving to know the causes at work in each event he witnesses" appears not only in higher civilizations but also among the lowest of primitive men. But unlike most of the older philosophers, he studies myth in great earnestness: "the old myths," he announces, "have fairly taken their place among historic facts." He believes he can show that they are solidly grounded in "the actual experience of nature and life." It will not do to dismiss them as unintelligible or accidental any more than it will to attribute them to the contrivance of priests or to talk vaguely about primitive poets.

Tylor's two principles in studying myth are "animism" and "analogy." Animism, which to Tylor has a more general application than to mythology, is "the belief in spiritual beings." [2] Animism is the doctrine (1) of souls and (2) of other spirits. The idea of the soul is derived from disembodied images seen in dreams, trances, hallucinations, or reflections in the water. The presence, the absence, the benevolence, the malevolence, the health, the sickness of souls is appealed to in the effort to understand and control those common phenomena of life which now are understood and controlled by science, especially medicine. Furthermore, primitive philosophy attributes spirits analogous to souls—in various stages of personification—to the inanimate objects of nature, and intelligence to animals, birds, and fishes. To the savage, the sun, trees, rivers, and clouds possess personal spirits; behind the terrible or pleasing operations of nature "there stands some prodigious but yet half human creature." Xerxes would scarcely have flogged the Hellespont had he not imagined himself flogging a spirit; in old English law the cart wheel which ran over a man or the tree which fell on him would not have been judged guilty if they had not been thought alive; nor would the household goods of a recently dead German peasant have been carefully shaken unless they were imagined to be capable of receiving the message that the master was dead.[3] The rainbow which the New Zealanders believed capable of destroying trees and which the Burmese accused of devouring men are other cases in point. These practices and beliefs, according to Tylor, are based on analogies: that is, objects are thought to feel and act in ways analogous to human feelings and actions. And not only does the mythopoeic mind make analogies between men and objects but also between different objects, as when the rainbow is said to be a bridge or when the Princess and her brother who live in the Peruvian sky make thunder by striking a vase full of rain. Most of the authors we have already discussed have agreed with Tylor that the habit of animating nature is in some sense fundamental to the creation of myth, but Tylor is the first to limit animation precisely to the "doctrine of souls." He will not allow the metaphors of primitive poets as the beginning of myth, for some of the analogies from which myth arises are "real and sensible" (here he would perhaps agree with Vico and his idea of "real words"); "material myth" is the primary formation; "verbal myth" is secondary. Myth is therefore *prelinguistic,* a fact which, as Tylor insists, the philologists have failed to understand.

In determining the psychological quality of primitive myth, Tylor tries to escape what Vico had called "the conceit of the learned," though as we shall see he has been justly accused of falling into this error.[4] Despite his wariness of poetic interpretations, he tells us that throwing one's mind back to "the world's older life" is the poet's gift and he applauds Max Müller for having observed that Wordsworth was especially endowed with this gift,[5] and Tylor uses the phrase "the poetic stage of thought." The mythopoeic mind, he says, has pre-eminently a "sense of the reality of ideas," a sense of immediate color and form of which our education has robbed us. "I have never forgotten," he writes, "the vividness with which, as a child, I fancied I might look through a great telescope, and see the constellations stand round the sky, red, green, and yellow, as I had just been shown them on the celestial globe. The intensity of mythic fancy may be brought even more nearly home to our minds by comparing it with the morbid subjectivity of illness. Among the lower races, and high above their level, morbid ecstasy brought on by meditation, fasting, narcotics, excitement, or disease, is a state common and held in honor among the very classes specially concerned with mythic idealism, and under its influence the barriers between sensation and imagination break utterly away." And Tylor records the ecstatic vision of an American Indian woman to whom a man appeared, announcing himself as "the Bright Blue Sky." Around his head was a bright halo; his breast was covered with squares; "but how far is our cold analysis," says Tylor, "from her utter belief that in vision she had really seen this bright being, this Red Indian Zeus." The appeal to the psychology of children and of ecstatics was not the most respectable kind of scientific procedure in Tylor's time; yet the Englishman who had steeped himself in *Alice in Wonderland* and was one day to applaud the psychology of William James must have attended closely to Tylor.[6] We should not forget these striking psychological insights when we call Tylor, what he generally is, a rationalist.

Tylor distinguishes two main classes of myth: (1) nature myths and (2) philosophic myths, though he does not always keep the distinction quite clear. Let us see what Tylor means by his two classes of myth.

(1) Tylor assures us that there is considerable ethnological support for the theory that mythology concerns the sun, the moon, the constellations, the seasons, the winds, clouds, and storms. "Direct conceptions of nature . . . are among the primary sources of myth." But Tylor is suspicious of the Max Müller school and will accept meteorological interpretations of myth only when the myths in question can be shown actually to be alive among primitive peoples. He demonstrates satirically that the "Song of Sixpence" can be taken as a meteorological myth and that a case can be made out for thinking that Julius Caesar was a sun-god. On the other hand the Algonquin hero Manabozho seems to be a genuine solar divinity; the Greek myths of Perseus and Andromeda and of Heracles and Hesione may well be descriptions of the Sun slaying the Darkness, and even Little Red Ridinghood is probably the Sun, and the wolf the Night. This last, he observes, is similar to the widespread story of the human being who is swallowed by a monster, a story found in the myth of Jonah and in various forms among the Ojibways, the Maoris, the Basutos, and the Zulus.

One of the most striking "nature myths" which Tylor records is the Maori version of the myth of heaven and earth. I quote this at some length (Tylor in turn is quoting Sir George Grey, who recorded the myth in 1850 in his *Polynesian Mythology*):

> From Rangi, the Heaven, and Papa, the Earth, it is said, sprang all men and things, but sky and earth clave together, and darkness rested upon them and the beings they had begotten, till at last their children took counsel whether they should rend apart their parents, or slay them. Then Tane-mahuta, father of forests, said to his five great brethren, "It is better to rend them apart, and to let the heaven stand far above us, and the earth lie under our feet. Let the sky become as a stranger to us, but the earth remain close to us as a nursing mother." So Rongo-ma-tane, god and father of the cultivated food of man, arose and strove to separate the heaven and the earth; he struggled but in vain, and vain too were the efforts of Tangaroa, father of fish and reptiles, and of Haumia-tikitiki, father of wild growing food, and of Tu-matauenga, god and father of fierce men. Then slow uprises Tane-mahuta, god and father of forests, and wrestles with his parents, striving to part them with his hands and arms. Lo, he pauses; his head is now firmly planted on his mother the earth, his feet he raises up and rests against his father the skies, he strains his back and limbs with mighty effort. Now are rent apart Rangi and Papa, and with cries and groans of woe they shriek aloud. . . . But Tane-mahuta pauses not; far, far beneath him he presses down the earth; far, far above him he thrusts up the sky. But Tawhiri-ma-tea, father of winds and storms, had never consented that his mother should be torn from her lord, and now arose in his breast a fierce desire to war against his brethren. [The rest of the myth concerns the eternal war of brother upon brother.]

To Tylor this story is a "simple nature myth," a dramatic description, partly poetic, partly explanatory, of the sky and the earth, which the Maori imagined to be motivated by half-human spirits. In other words the Maori made the myth by contemplating nature and explaining its operations in terms of human relationships; this view doubtless has an element of truth; yet it remains the one-sided interpretation of the nineteenth-century scientist and nature worshiper. The myth is remarkably like the hypothetical story (itself a myth) of the origin of society in Freud's "Totem and Taboo," but we do not need Freud to see in this myth human relationships primarily and sky, earth, and storms secondarily. Surely it cannot be a "simple nature myth," for it dramatizes some of the most primitive and profound of human emotions.

(2) Under the head of "philosophic myths" Tylor places those

in which we see most plainly the primitive man's "craving to know causes." Thus the stories to be found in *The Arabian Nights,* in certain medieval poems, and in Mandeville, which tell of ships being irresistibly pulled toward a magnetic mountain, or of the nails drawn out of ships by the power of magnetism, are myths composed to account for the behavior of the compass needle. Myths concerning the degeneration of men into apes or the metamorphosis of apes into men, to be found among the Zulus and in Central America, Southern India, and on the Malay peninsula, are examples of primitive anthropological speculation. Myths about giants may be attempted explanations of fossil bones. Myths about dwarfs, men with no noses, men with one eye, men with ears so large they are used for blankets, men with heads like dogs, men with no heads, men whose feet are turned in opposite directions, are stories invented to account for falsely reported human peculiarities. Heroic myths may be invented to account for the ruins of ancient buildings or for watercourses: both Heracles and Alexander were said to have opened the Straits of Gibraltar. Myths may be etymological: Exeter is said to have got its name from the cry of *"Ecce terra!"* which the Romans uttered when they first beheld the place where the city now stands. Certain myths may be eponymic: according to mythical history the four sons of Japhet were Francus, Romanus, Alemannus, and Britto, heroes invented to account for the founding of nations with corresponding names. All of these "philosophic myths" appear, as Tylor presents them to us, to be a sort of childish pseudo science; they explain things which we have learned to explain better by means of physics, anthropology, biology, or history.

The reader will gather from the kinds of myths Tylor selects and from his attitude toward them that the author of *Primitive Culture* suffered from the limitations of his time. His faith in Victorian science and the Victorian idea of progress was very great. This faith entails an overestimation of the rationalism of primitive man and an underestimation of the stability of primitive psychology and morals. To Tylor the American Indian is enslaved by "absurd belief and useless ceremony"; he is a childlike creature of whimsical moods, subject to fits of insanity; the slightest occasion may drive him suddenly to the most bestial cruelty or the most meaningless folly.[7] In other words, though the savage is capable of rational (if mistaken) scientific thought, he is always on the verge of insanity. He is a kind of insane rationalist, like the mad scientists of popular fiction. This is the judgment of the armchair anthropologist. There is thus a damaging cleavage in Tylor's idea of primitive mentality. Another cleavage is also damaging: Tylor speaks of the craving of the mythmaking mind for philosophical explanation as "an intellectual appetite whose satisfaction claims many of the moments not engrossed by war or sport, food or sleep." He thinks of the making of myths as a speculative function *apart from* the ordinary pursuits of life. Until a more pragmatic method had been developed, this one-sided idea could not be corrected. Indeed some of the older writers we have considered were in advance of Tylor on this point.

Tylor's achievement remains, however, a great one. He had all the considerable virtues of the rationalist-evolutionary school of thinkers and some not commonly associated with that school. His *Primitive Culture* had the rough majesty and the imposing intellectualism of its author. But two of Tylor's contemporaries were able to bring to the study of myth something of what Tylor lacked. Herbert Spencer, despite his astonishing abstractions, was more accurate than Tylor in his strictures on primitive mentality if not in his more positive suggestions. And Andrew Lang was somewhat more sensitive to literature than Tylor, and this made him a more flexible and sensitive mythologist.

3.

Like Tylor, Herbert Spencer seeks the origin of the mythopoeic psychology in the savage's empirical observation of a dual universe: a universe of objects and a universe of spirits or ghosts. But unlike Tylor, he thinks that the savage is neither rational nor curious; he may even be described as stupid, apathetic—"at first an almost passive recipient of conclusions forced on him." [8] The constant mutations, the appearances and disappearances to be observed in the sky and on earth indicate to the savage that things have two existences: the sun is sometimes here and now; but sometimes it lives in another realm of being. A sleeping man is in one place but in his dreams he goes elsewhere—"for the primitive man regards a dream as a series of actual occurrences." The dreamer's ghost lives a life

separate from that of the dreamer; if a man swoons or falls unconscious his ghost is considered to have left him temporarily; if he
dies it has gone permanently. But, says Spencer, there is no question
of primitive philosophy here; the savages simply accept what seem
to be the facts without questioning or trying to explain. The ghosts
of men arouse a sense of fear and religious awe, and the impulse to
placate them and enlist their help or pity is the beginning of religion. The ghosts of great warriors and leaders are naturally the
most awesome and these gather to themselves the religious emotions
one attaches to the ghosts of one's own ancestors, thus becoming
tribal ancestors, the official deities of the tribe. At first thought of
as being exactly like men, in need of food, mortal, punishable by
force, the ghosts achieve a gradual apotheosis, losing some of their
human characteristics and finally becoming "etherialized." The sun,
the moon, idols, animals, plants, natural powers and causes are only
secondarily objects of worship and acquire their sanctity only by being identified in one way or another—often by mistaken etymologies—with deified ancestors.

The Greek gods are no exception to the general rule. Nothing,
says Spencer, is so much insisted upon by the Greeks as the humanness of their gods and the eagerness of the gods to appear among
men and to live like men. Spencer observes that several Greek gods—
in company with a Fijian deity—are called "the Adulterer"; Zeus
is called "the Woman-stealer"; a Fijian god is called "Fresh-from-
the-Slaughter," as Ares is called "the Blood-stainer." Does not Helen
berate Aphrodite? Does not Laomedon refuse to pay Poseidon his
wages and threaten to cut off his ears? Are not the gods wounded
by men's weapons and even, like Ares, kept in jail by mortals? The
gods are perpetually "running down from Olympus"; they are always reverting to the human world whence they sprang. Spencer
is, as we can see, a thoroughgoing euhemerist.

Despite the great differences between them, Max Müller and
Tylor agree on the general proposition that religion and myth originate in large part from man's contemplation of nature. Now just
as Hume's euhemerism was salutary in his day so was Spencer's in
his, for it set him apart from the dogma of his time and allowed
him—despite the crudeness of his own system—to make valuable
criticisms of other systems. What of the battles in heaven which we

find in Indian, Greek, Babylonian, Tibetan, Polynesian, and Christian mythologies? asks Spencer. Are they allegorical battles of the elements as the philologists say? Are they stories composed to explain the origin of the cosmos or the genesis of mankind, as Tylor says? Surely not. "They are expanded and idealized stories of human transactions"—there were battles on earth before it occurred to men to suppose that there were battles in heaven. No more than civilized children do primitive men wonder at the order of nature or even at its appearance. They are content to accept the universe, only being interested or terrified by some extraordinary occurrence. And such an occurrence does not arouse philosophy in them but rather turns their minds toward the most interesting of things, human life, and that most awe-inspiring of things, the death of a man and the activities of his ghost. Finally, says Spencer, primitive man has neither the imagination nor the intelligence the Nature Mythologists ascribe to him. Here we must agree with Spencer, though we may wish that he had also said that we *do not have to assume* these accomplishments in order to explain mythology, instead of dogmatizing—in company with the Nature Mythologists—about the mind of primitive man.

Spencer's larger sociological generalizations are not very agreeable to modern thought. But euhemerism in the hands of an intelligent thinker is always a beneficial astringent when more grandiose intellectual and poetical theories go unchallenged. The euhemerist attitude, though euhemerism is not to be accepted as a generally adequate theory, holds that the materials and purposes of myth are stubbornly human, a truth perceived, as we have noticed, by the intuitive poetic historians Vico and Herder, and insisted upon by Hume.

4.

Andrew Lang was a student of nearly everything that could be studied in the late Victorian period. He wrote in every known form—poems, treatises, essays, lectures—and he usually wrote with wit and elegance. He was a *philosophe* in the manner of Fontenelle—a popular propagandist in favor of Reason and Tolerance. Mythology was one of his abiding interests and Max Müller was his favorite target (we have indicated above the general tenor of Lang's antiphilological criticism). Lang early declared himself an adherent of the anthropological method as it was set forth by Tylor and Spencer, though he found far less to praise in Spencer than in Tylor. We know that Lang proclaimed Fontenelle his master in the study of mythology, and indeed his major work on this subject, *Myth, Ritual and Religion,* is in a sense Fontenelle's *Origin of Fables* brought up to date. During most of his life Lang was a thorough-going evolutionist; yet his break with the evolutionist theory constitutes his most memorable achievement. But of that later.

Lang begins with the familiar rationalist idea that man has always been eager to know the causes of things and that the mythology of primitive man is a philosophy of nature based on animism.[9] In his *Myth, Ritual and Religion,* he speaks of myth evolving out of "savage metaphysics" and "savage science," of primitive man's "need for making the world intelligible." Primitive man, says Lang, is boundlessly curious and also boundlessly credulous, willing to take the first answer he hears, no matter how fantastic or obscene, to the question his curiosity propounds. In order to understand myth we must uncover that ancient stratum in history of which it is the product, as the biologist reconstructs history by studying fossils. At one time fossil bones were working parts of animals, and though they may seem strange, archaic, or monstrous now, they did not seem so then. In the study of myth we must ask ourselves, "Is there a stage of human society and of the human intellect in which facts that appear to us to be monstrous and irrational—facts corresponding to the incidents of myth—are accepted as ordinary occurrences?" Was there a time, in other words, when myths which seem to us perplexing or irrational were taken to be rational? Lang's answer to this question is "Yes." Following Tylor, he believes that this ancient stage of society, which can still be found in a greater or lesser degree of purity among modern primitive peoples, is animistic. The predominant philosophy of the time, Lang supposes, is based upon the idea of souls and spirits. If I understand him aright, however, Lang's notion of primitive psychology is more mystical than Tylor's. His idea of "that nebulous and confused frame of mind to which all things, animate or inanimate, human, animal, vegetable or inorganic seem to be on the same level of life, passion and reason" approaches what French anthropologists such as Lévy-Bruhl call *"participation mystique,"* that state of bemused subjectivism which they (mistakenly) suppose primitive man to be in. Again, Lang says that "the dead and the living, men, beasts and gods, trees and stars, and rivers, and sun, and moon, dance through the region of myths in a burlesque *ballet* of Priapus, where everything may be anything, where nature has no laws and imagination no limits." It is difficult to see what we gain by calling this *Walpurgisnacht* "savage science." But Lang is willing to be inconsistent.

As was the case with Tylor, the myths which interest Lang first are the ones which explain natural phenomena or the origin of things. How does the Australian account for the daily journey of the sun? The myth tells us that once it was always day, but men grew weary and longed for night. The god Norralie commanded the sun to burn up his supply of wood, and ever since, the sun has had to go below the horizon every night for fresh firewood. Other stories, from the Pacific and North America, say that the sun once traveled too fast and had to be snared and beaten so that he became lame and has ever since limped across the sky. Some myths, says Lang, account for the origin of species. The Greeks said that frogs were herdsmen metamorphosed by Leto; the Australians say frogs were once cattle who were beaten and driven into the water by a woman. The Australians say "the good spirit" Moora-Moora took some lizards, divided their feet into fingers and toes, cut off their tails so they could stand up, and thus made them into men; the Digger Indians of California have a myth describing the gradual development of coyotes into men. Various peoples have thought that the earth was originally an animal, or an egg, or a turtle, or a lump of mud fished out of the waters; man is said to have been made out of clay or a stone, or to have appeared in his present form out of a hole in the ground. Among the Hurons, as among the Greeks and other peoples, men were thought to have descended from a titanic race of superior beings; sometimes these beings are human in form; sometimes they are hares or wolves. Thus Lang supposed that many myths were invented by primitive cosmologists or savage Darwinians.

Unlike Tylor, Lang stresses the importance to mythology of magic, the science (as Lang describes it) which assumes that ideas and the associations into which they enter in the minds of men are faithful transcripts of cause and effect and other relations in the objective world. The medicine men, who claim control over the elements and the metamorphoses of species, are very like the gods and heroes of mythology. But here Lang makes it clear that he does not accept the euhemerist doctrine, which might say that the gods are nothing but medicine men made divine. (Spencer had in fact maintained that Aesculapius was a deified medicine man and that many such were to be found in various parts of the world.) [10]

Lang also makes totemism figure much larger in the creation of myths than had Tylor; he thinks that a great number of myths were invented to explain the origin and function of the totemic social system. And he suggests in his *Custom and Myth* that the story of Cupid and Psyche, which has analogues in various parts of the world, was composed to explain one of those widespread taboos which forbade the wife to see her husband naked, to look upon his face at certain times, to utter his name, or to touch him with certain substances, such as metal. Like Tylor, Lang is far more interested in cosmogonic and biological myths than in such heroic myths as those of Jason and Hercules. Nor do the universal folk tales which tell of beasts and children and heroes and monsters claim as much of his attention as we should like—though, as we shall see in the next chapter, he does turn to them late in life.

Andrew Lang's peculiar contribution to the study of mythology, however, is his idea that even the lowest of savages worship a "high god" and that if this is so mythology must be reconsidered.[11] The traditional evolutionist view, maintained in modern times by such thinkers as Fontenelle, Hume, de Brosses, Herder, Darwin, Tylor, and Spencer, holds of course that religion began with what Hume called a "familiar and grovelling notion of superior powers"—that it passed from a worship of fetishes or spirits into polytheism and thence to monotheism, which in enlightened times tends to broaden out into deism or theism. Evolution denies any kind of ethical theism to savages. Tylor believed that morality and religion were originally separate—a sound Victorian dissenting position but one maintained in all times by the skeptical but ethical mind. "Looking at religion from a political point of view, as a practical influence on human society," Tylor writes, "it is clear that among its greatest powers has

been its divine sanction of ethical laws. . . . But such alliance belongs almost or wholly to religions above the savage level, not to
the earlier and lower creeds." [12] With this Lang does not agree: the
Australians and the Andamanese, he says, practice charity and
righteousness, and their high gods sanction these virtues.

Lang observes that the interpretation of myth has traditionally
been a moral problem. As soon as a nation attained some philosophy
it began to observe that the gods of its myths were immoral. Philosophers and poets could not always accept the cruelties and ob-
scenities of the old myths and so tried to reconcile them to a higher
moral code, by ignoring them as Homer sometimes did, by refusing
to believe them (as when Pindar in his *Olympic Odes* refuses to say
that the blessed gods were cannibals), or by reading exalted moral
allegories into them as did the Stoics. On the other hand, the Greeks
as well as other peoples found that the nonmythological elements
of their traditional religion contained much that was pure and
ethical. These same interpreters of myth, Lang writes, found a
similar cleavage in their religious tradition between the "rational"
and the "irrational." They found traditions of certain wise and
benevolent beings who taught men the arts of life, such as language
or the use of fire, and these traditions seemed perfectly rational, as
well as moral. But side by side with these rational traditions were
myths which described the same wise and benevolent beings as rab-
bits, dogs, or spiders. The Olympian Zeus of the noble statues or the
Homeric Zeus who protects the righteous was also the god "who
played Demeter an obscene trick by the aid of a ram," or the god
who made love in the shape of a swan, an ant, or a cuckoo, as Kronos
and Poseidon made love disguised as horses. Thus, Lang tells us, "the
whole crux and puzzle of mythology" has always been and still is
"Why, having attained . . . to a belief in an undying guardian,
'Master of Life,' did mankind set to work to evolve a *chronique
scandaleuse* about Him? And why is that *chronique* the elaborately
absurd set of legends which we find in all mythologies?"

To begin with, Lang says that there has always been an essential
conflict between religion and myth—not only in advanced cultures
but among all peoples, even the lowest. The evolutionists say that
in the earliest times religion and mythology are essentially the same
thing, but to Lang—and he calls this "the main theory" of his

book—"religion is one thing, myth quite another." [13] He believes
this to be true even among the lowly Australians; and among the yet
lower Andamanese there is an "extraordinary contradiction between
the relative purity and morality of the religion and the savagery of
the myths." [14] But we should remember that Lang's distinction
between myth and religion depends on his rather narrow definition
of religion as moral theism. Now the high gods of certain very primitive people, Lang says, are "moral and creative deities"; they are
"existences," "beings." Unlike the mythological gods, they are "un-
conditioned," "unborn and not subject to death"—though they
have anthropomorphic mythical counterparts like "the gigantic
black, once on earth now among the stars" of the Australians, or
theriomorphic counterparts like Cagn, the Great Grasshopper of
the African Bushmen. These moral, theistic beings have nothing in
common with spirits and ghosts; furthermore, they are worshiped
among people who do not worship either spirits or ghosts. This being
so, Lang writes, the theories of Tylor and Spencer about the origin
of religion will have to be abandoned, and the evolutionary account
of religion will have to make way for the new facts. Lang believes
that though there are myths among the lowest peoples, myth is more
characteristic of a second, less moral and less rational stage of society.
Does he then accept all over again the theory of degeneration? In this
matter he is noncommittal. He does indeed sometimes speak of degeneration, but he disclaims the idea of an original revelation. Usually he is purely pragmatic: his theory, he says, is the one which
"colligates the facts"; probably "any race of men may be called
monotheistic, just as, in another sense, Christians who revere saints
may be called polytheistic . . . whenever man turns to a guardian
not of this world, not present to the senses, man is for the moment
a theist, and often a monotheist. But when we look from aspiration
to doctrine, from the solitary ejaculation to ritual, from religion to
myth, it would probably be vain to suppose that an uncontaminated
belief in one god only, the maker and creator of all things, has generally prevailed, either in America or elsewhere." This was an insight
which seemed more and more fruitful to students of religion and
mythology as the shackles of evolution were gradually loosened,
though in Lang's time it was received with hostility or silence.

We are now in a better position to observe how Lang answers the

question, "Why have men all over the world composed myths?" He
has two answers: his first is the familiar answer of the rationalist; but
his second is pragmatic. Lang's rationalism was modified in later life
by his reading of William James, Charcot, and Janet, all of whom
exerted an influence on his book *The Making of Religion* (1898).
He tells us in this book that myths were created to fulfill certain profound emotional needs which religion could not satisfy:

> "How," it has been asked, "could all mankind forget a pure
> religion?" [15] That is what I now try to explain. That degeneration
> I would account for by the attractions which animism, when once
> developed, possessed for the naughty natural man, "the old Adam."
> A moral creator in need of no gifts, and opposed to lust and mischief,
> will not help a man with love-spells, or with malevolent "sendings"
> of disease by witchcraft; will not favor one man above his neighbor,
> or one tribe above its rivals, as a reward for sacrifice which he does
> not accept, or as constrained by charms which do not touch his
> omnipotence. Ghosts and ghost-gods, on the other hand, in need of
> food and blood, afraid of spells and binding charms, are a corrupt,
> but to a man, a useful constituency. Man being what he is, man was
> certain to "go a-whoring" after practically useful ghosts, ghost-
> gods, and fetishes which he could keep in his wallet or medicine bag.
> For these he was sure, in the long run, first to neglect his idea of his
> creator; next, perhaps, to reckon him as only one, if the highest, of
> the venal rabble of spirits or deities, and to sacrifice to Him, as to
> them. . . .

It is refreshing to find rationalism abandoning its principles and ad-
mitting that myth may be explained as the fulfillment of man's desire
for "practically useful ghosts." This simple truth was traditionally
obscured by the tendency to regard myth exclusively as useless absurdity or exclusively as a species of intellection.

Lang's account of the evolution of Zeus may help us to bring
together the confessedly somewhat scattered fragments of his degeneration hypothesis—always remembering that to Lang it was only a
hypothesis. Zeus, then, may once have been the moral, the omnipotent, the eternal sky-god whose rule over mortals was absolute. And
so he is sometimes portrayed in Greek poetry; but he is also portrayed
as subject to all the frailties and follies of mankind and even of animals (we find that *the myths* about Zeus were more faithfully preserved in mystery plays, genealogies, and village traditions of the
kind gathered by Pausanias than in Greek poetry). Lang praises

Otfried Müller for insisting that the local myths of Greece are the most ancient and the most enlightening. He believes that the Greek conception of Zeus degenerated "while Greece was reaching a general national consciousness, and becoming more than an aggregate of small local tribes." This degeneration occurred when each tribe attached its own folklore, its own genealogies, and especially its own totems to the name of Zeus or retold its myths so as to include Zeus. And this explains why such a confusing array of scientific, etiological, and imaginative myths are told about Zeus. The old high Zeus was too austere and distant for men engaged in the struggle of life and he was accordingly degraded into a multitude of "practically useful ghosts." However true or false a picture this may be of Greek history or of religious evolution in general, it seems incontrovertibly true as a statement of the difference between religion, regarded as theism, and myth. And it demonstrates what Tylor denied: that the irrational, the mythical, has a profound utility in human life.

To students of myth Andrew Lang is a crucial figure; for he brings us back to the central problems. In his work we see the end of the nineteenth century's exclusive preoccupation with nature myths. He did more than any of his contemporaries to show the limits of the first-rate philologists and the errors of the second-rate. Starting out from Tylor's rational-evolutionist position, he gradually rejected that too—though only tentatively and reluctantly. But once we begin, with Lang, to talk of the pragmatic function of myth, and to loosen the psychological bonds of rationalism, we are back with Hume, Vico, and Herder. And we are ready to go forward to the anthropologists and psychoanalysts—who clarify some of the problems which remain unsolved.[16]

CHAPTER VI

MYTH AND MODERN
ANTHROPOLOGY

THE THINKERS we have so far considered in this book
have nearly all made monistic judgments about the savage and
his society. The primitive mind was said to be poetic, philosophical, scientific, or subjective. Primitive man was described as stupid
or the master of recondite lore. He was atheistic or he was
utterly enthralled with ritual or dogmatic religion. He displayed
perpetual curiosity about the universe or he displayed no curiosity,
contenting himself with an apathetic acceptance of things as they
are. He was bestial or noble. Whatever quality a particular writer
chose to attribute to primitive man, he usually attributed it to *all*
primitive men, so that primitive society appeared to be an undif-
ferentiated embodiment of the quality. Those few writers, such as
Creuzer and Voltaire, who tried to point out the difference between
the psychic and the social functions of the priests and those of the
people were not taken seriously; nor did they have the facts at hand
to support their theories. The traditional monistic descriptions of
savage society are to be accounted for by the writer's peculiar polemical purpose, or, most important, by his particular theories of
evolution or cyclical development, which demanded clear-cut,
homogeneous stages of society and blinded him to the variations
within primitive society.

The modern anthropologists agree [1] in accepting no general uni-
lateral theory of cultural evolution, though in practice some of them
do fall back on the older theories. They agree that no existing society can be regarded as preserving the primordial state of things.
They tend to be suspicious of the comparative method and they

have shown that this method, as it was employed by Tylor, Spencer, and Frazer, has only a limited utility, since it considers only a limited number of phenomena which are widespread or universal and since it can easily misrepresent the significance of any particular custom or belief by failing to consider it in its cultural context.

Modern anthropologists insist that primitive societies, in varying degrees, allow for differences in temperament; they show that individualists exist in societies once thought to be homogeneous and that these individualists sometimes exert a fundamental influence on their fellows. Paul Radin is the writer who has shown most exhaustively the implications of temperamental variations. His *Primitive Man as Philosopher* describes the relationship between "the man of action" and "the man of thought," two classes which we sometimes call in our own society "the masses" and "the intelligentsia." In his *Primitive Religion* [2] Radin shows the error of supposing that primitive men are uniformly religious. Truly religious men, he says, "have always been few in number"; most men have always been but "indifferently" or "intermittently" religious. The layman is a rough-and-ready pragmatist who is likely to attribute religious qualities to that which works. As Radin says, "it was no religious man who, among the Maori, insisted that gods die unless there are priests to keep them alive." [3] It will be useful in studying mythology to remember that, if Radin is right, the ordinary savage believes in spirits because of the effects they produce and that since he looks at effects rather than causes, the spirits, to him, are likely to assume no very clear personification but remain plastic and undefined. [4] The influence of the pragmatic savage is counterbalanced in a number of ways, which we will discuss later, by his temperamental opposite, the priest-thinker, whose business it is to systematize the religious emotions of the people, to establish the identity and integrity of deities, sometimes to evolve a pantheon, or, if he is able to secure enough leisure, to speculate about man and the universe. [5]

Since Tylor's day the idea of primitive religion has been radically revised. Tylor's "minimum definition of religion" as a "belief in spiritual beings" was soon found to be inadequate. For the idea that the savage in a state of religious emotion conceived of a particular spirit dwelling in whatever object he was contemplating does not account for the prerational dynamism of religious acts, a fact which was often noticed before Tylor—by Hume, de Brosses, Vico, Herder, and others. Later students have observed that Tylor neglected that vastly important substratum of religious life—magic. The greatest modern codifier of magical lore is of course Sir James Frazer. To Frazer magic "is a false science," a "spurious system of natural law." Magic, he says, works on two principles: "the Law of Similarity" and "the Law of Contact and Contagion." "From the first of these principles . . . the magician infers that he can produce any effect he desires merely by imitating it: from the second he infers that whatever he does to a material object will affect equally the person with whom the object was once in contact." [6] Frazer supposed that magic was the first stage of human thought and that it was succeeded by religion—a fundamentally different way of looking at the world, for whereas the magician believes in his own ability to set the invariable chain of natural cause and effect into operation, the religious man believes he must propitiate spirits or gods, whose intervention in the operations of nature or the affairs of the world he implores.[7] Thus religion is a kind of postponement of the arrival of the third and ultimate human discipline: true science. This schematic arrangement undoubtedly represents a profound truth, and it proves adequate as a framework for *The Golden Bough.* Yet the best opinion now makes three basic objections to it: (1) no uniform and universal evolution of magic to religion to science can be demonstrated; (2) magic and religion, while undoubtedly different, cannot be separated as sharply from each other as Frazer thought; (3) Frazer's definitions are too abstract and so do not sufficiently recognize the emotional, compulsive character of magic.

One of the best writers on magic and religion is R. R. Marett, the successor of Tylor at Oxford and Tylor's biographer.[8] In his *The Threshold of Religion* he supplements Tylor's theory of animism with a theory of "preanimism." The substratum of "the belief in spiritual beings" he equates with what Frazer had called the magic stage of thought. He suggests that the psychology of this substratum be called "animatism," or the belief that certain objects have a mysterious potency *as part of themselves* and not because they contain a spirit. He does not deny that religion may evolve from magic but he sees more to be gained by thinking of magic and religion as two parts of one whole.[9]

To modern anthropologists the basic principle of the primitive's magico-religious world is what the Melanesian peoples call *mana*, a principle of which Frazer gives no satisfactory account.[10] *Mana* is usually thought to be a universal principle among primitive peoples, occurring among various tribes under such names as *orenda*, *maxpé*, and *oki*. As we have seen above, de Brosses and Rousseau apprehended this principle under the name of *manitou*, and Vico under the name of Jupiter; Herder identified it by such German words as *Wirkung*, and Hume by such English words as "power" and "vitality." Magic is now thought to be the compulsive technique of setting *mana* into operation in one's own interest. A precise definition of *mana*, as one might expect, is difficult to formulate, and different writers give differing definitions. It can perhaps be best understood if we consider it under three closely related categories: (1) the dynamic, (2) the aesthetic-dynamic, and (3) the incipiently conceptual. (1) Thus Professor A. O. Lovejoy believes that things are said to be mysterious, wonderful, or awful—to have *mana*—*because* they are "efficacious, powerful, productive." [11] *Mana*, he thinks, is a "persuasive, life-giving, impersonal energy" and things which have *mana* become beautiful or terrific because they produce effects. (2) Marett gives a less militantly pragmatic definition. He considers *mana*, to be sure, as "supernatural power," as "voltage," as a "mystic potentiality"; but he insists that though "*mana* is often operative and thaumaturgic," it is not always so. Sometimes *mana* may impress the savage immediately as a quality—awfulness, mysteriousness, beauty—while, as an operative force, it may remain dormant. A corpse, says Marett, is universally admitted to have *mana;* but what seems immediately important to the native is not the potential activity of the ghost but "the awfulness felt to attach to the dead human body in itself." Professor Benedict agrees that *mana* is an "impersonal force." [12] But, even more than Marett, she insists that it is an immediately apprehended quality: the primitive "saw this supernatural [13] quality as an attribute of objects just as color and weight are attributes of objects." (3) We should expect that for those who imagine spirits or gods *mana* might hover between the impersonal and the personal, that it might sometimes be conceptualized. Thus the word *manitou* appears in both impersonal and personal gender in the Algonquin language.[14] Temperamental differences appear in primitive ideas of *mana* as well as elsewhere: Radin says that while *mana* to the layman was "magical potency, that which worked, had activity, was an effect," to the priest-thinker it might be "the generalized essence of a deity residing in an object or in man."[15]

It is generally agreed that, given the substratum of magic, religion is indeed "the belief in spiritual beings." Marett says that the idea of spirits comes from the ghosts of the dead and that these take on shape and color by analogy with the beings envisioned in dreams and trances.[16] In the words of Professor Benedict,[17] spirits inhabit a wonderful wish world fashioned on the pattern of human will and intention. The religious—as opposed to the magical—technique of dealing with this wish world is not, of course, compulsion but rapport, propitiation, sacrifice, prayer. Thus in its simplest formulation the primitive magico-religious world may be said to comprise animatism, "the belief in *mana*," and animism, "the belief in spirits."

The older theorists thought of religion either as a divine revelation apart from the life of the world or as an egregious error which perpetually distracted men from social or intellectual improvement by interfering with secular activities. Modern anthropologists, however, assert the social function of religion. Radin thinks that religion is "the emotional correlate of the struggle for existence in an insecure physical and social environment." It has a positive, beneficial effect: "it emphasizes and preserves those values accepted by the majority of a group at a given time."[18] Radin even endeavors to socialize the emotion of fear, which so many writers have found to be the first religious emotion. To Radin, fear is indeed fundamental in religion, but he believes the savage fears nature and death much less than he fears hunger and the cruelty of the chief or priest.[19] The savage himself believes in the social function of religion: as the Winnebago Indians say, the spirits help one through "the crises and narrow places of life."[20]

Modern anthropology has disclosed the infinite variations from tribe to tribe of belief and custom. There have been so many studies of single cultures, usually pointing out the differences among cultures rather than the similarities, that the total picture they give us is bewildering indeed. The tendency among anthropologists is to think of all primitive societies as potentially possessing in common a vague body of folklore concerning ghosts, gods, spirits, magic, witchcraft, sorcery, practical knowledge, customs and beliefs of all sorts. Each society, for reasons mostly inscrutable, has chosen a certain segment of this folklore and repressed the remainder.[21] The history of this process is very seldom ascertainable and many writers prefer to remain resolutely skeptical about it. The traditional theory about the influence of the climate, maintained by Montesquieu and Herder, does not always help.[22] And though religion always has a social function, it is not necessarily the one we might expect. For an agricultural people may have a religion which has nothing to do with the fertility of the crops; a hunting people may have a religion that has nothing to do with hunting; facts which should give pause to those who embrace rigid utilitarian theories of religion and rite.[23] R. H. Lowie says that "cultures are not so much set off from one another by distinctive traits as by the weighting and organization of these traits into a distinctive whole." Lowie distinguishes the religion of any one tribe in a purely psychological manner—by trying to learn what arouses the savage's sense of the "Extraordinary." [24] Radin looks for an explanation of a particular religion in the economic situation behind it and in the temperament of the person who has won economic control. The neurotic shaman impresses his personality on the religion of the Siberians and on that of many of the American Indians; the medicine man imposes a primarily magical religion on his fellows; and the priest a primarily ceremonial religion on his. Our knowledge of the history of primitive society is obviously too incomplete to support any final theory of cultural determinism.

The great fact with which modern anthropology has confronted us is the enormous diversity of culture, ranging all the way from a tribe such as the Dobuans,[25] whose life is almost entirely bound up in magic and who consequently have few if any clearly definable gods, to the Maori,[26] who have a pantheon in some ways rivaling the Greek and whose philosophers developed a system of thought akin to the monadology of Leibnitz.

2.

With a few notable exceptions, the writers we have so far considered thought of myth as philosophy. Vico and Herder tell us that myth is poetic philosophy; Fontenelle, Tylor, and Lang tell us it is scientific philosophy. Nearly all of our writers agree that in early times myth and religion are next to indistinguishable and that myth is a kind of religious philosophy. Furthermore, nearly all of our writers tell us that myth was born out of primitive man's fear and adoration of nature or out of his curiosity concerning nature. Those authors who have accepted the degeneration theory of history tell us that myth is or was once an esoteric metaphysical or allegorical philosophy; [27] the evolutionists tell us that myth is a crude, false philosophy. Hume observed that "the vulgar" do not philosophize about the universe and Otfried Müller chose not to study cosmogonic myths because, in his estimation (no doubt an *over*estimation) these represented only 10 per cent of Greek myths. Nevertheless for most of our authors myth was pre-eminently philosophical, and the reader of these pages must often have felt that this preoccupation came more and more to exclude some of the most interesting and fruitful problems of mythology.

One such problem is posed by John Dewey: "Myths," he writes, "were something other than intellectualistic essays of primitive man in science . . . delight in the story . . . played its dominant part then as it does in the growth of popular mythologies today. Not only does the direct sense element . . . tend to absorb all ideational matter but . . . it subdues and digests all that is merely intellectual." Mythology, says Dewey, "is much more an affair of the psychology that generates art than an effort at scientific and philosophical explanation." [28] The American anthropologists agree with Dewey in discounting the philosophical function of myth. Those who stress the importance of exceptional individuals think that the philosophical ideas in mythology were imposed by individual thinkers upon already existing myths of the people, which were simply imaginary tales about human life.[29] They do not deny what the nineteenth-century thinkers insisted upon: that some myths give philosophical explanations of nature, of the origin of the world, of the migrations of sun, moon, and stars. When we look superficially from mythology to mythology these concepts are likely to strike us as the only stable element of myth. But it is a great mistake—the mistake of the comparative method—to assume, because a handful of philosophical concepts and explanations are relatively clearcut and appear in many different mythologies, that these are fundamentally characteristic of myth. A close examination of one culture area (a group of tribes who have exerted cultural influence on one another and who possess certain cultural elements in common) shows that the fundamental myth is the dramatic human tale. It is the philosophical explanations which appear to be unstable when we notice that different tribes may tell the same story but that in one case it is explanatory and in five or six other cases it is not.[30] Even within the same tribe a dramatic tale may be told of a mother, father, uncle, and children who in one version are purely human while in another version they acquire some of the characteristics of the moon, the sun, and the stars.[31] In many such semi-celestial tales there is no philosophizing or explanation but only an aesthetic solicitation of nature by a storyteller of a particular and probably unusual temperament. Boas appears to state the general view of the American anthropologists when he concludes that to interpret the myths which have been collected from the primitive mythmakers themselves "as a reflection of the observation of nature is obviously not justifiable." [32] The Crow Indians will tell you that their Great Being is the Sun. But they are extremely vague and confused as to his characteristics. He is always merging with that much more tangible deity, Old Man Coyote, the Crow culture hero.[33] "The Sun" is an extrusion, a mostly useless rationalization. Is it entirely reasonable to assume that all men, like many nineteenth-century philosophers, are more interested in nature than in themselves?

The older writers now seem to us to have neglected a simple and fundamental truth: *the word "myth" means story: a myth is a tale,*[34] *a narrative, or a poem; myth is literature and must be considered as an aesthetic creation of the human imagination.* A myth need be no more philosophical than any other kind of literature. In one sense we may say that there is no such thing as *a* myth, but only poetical stories which are more or less mythical; we may, however, call a story or tale which is primarily mythical a "myth" and we may use "story" or "tale" for a narrative which is not primarily mythical.

As soon as we begin to think of myth as literature there are three immediate questions to be answered. Are there any primitive peoples who have myths but no literature? What kinds of literature do primitive peoples have? What are the relations between them?

The answer to the first question is that no people has ever been known to be without a literature. Tales and songs are world-wide, writes Professor Boas. "The Bushman and the Eastern Eskimo, although poor in the production of art, are rich in tales and songs, of which they possess a well-nigh inexhaustible treasure. The poor hunter of the Malay peninsula and the Australians have their literature no less than economically more advanced people. Songs and tales are found all over the world. These are the fundamental forms of literature among primitive people." [35] In fairness to the older students of myth we must observe here that the universality of primitive literature had become known only to the relatively recent collectors of folklore, who, following the example of the brothers Grimm, have brought together an overwhelming body of folk literature from both primitive and civilized countries. [36]

The division of Greek mythological literature made by Heyne and Herder has become more or less standard in modern times. Sir James Frazer carries this division to its logical conclusion. *Myths proper*, he writes, are concerned with the origin of the world and man, the motions of the stars, the vicissitudes of vegetation, weather, eclipses, storms, the discovery of fire, the invention of the useful arts, the mystery of death. *Legends* are "traditions, whether oral or written, which relate the fortunes of real people in the past, or which describe events, not necessarily human, that are said to have occurred at real places." *Folk tales* are "purely imaginary, having no other aim than the entertainment of the hearer and making no real claim on his credulity." Frazer refers to the stories of Meleager, Melampus, Medea, Glaucus, Perseus, Peleus, Thetis, and Polyphemus as folk tales. [37] Malinowski makes a similar division in his "Myth in Primitive Psychology," [38] pointing out that he is following a division made by the natives themselves (the Trobriand Islanders).

Some American anthropologists appear to suppose that the literary categories made by certain American Indian tribes as well as by the

Greeks and other peoples are generally applicable. Myths, according to this formulation, are tales relating to a past mythological age, when the world was different from its present state. Folk tales are stories of present or of recent events.[39] (To the anthropologists "legends" apparently do not emerge as a clear category, being absorbed into myth or folk tale. It is no doubt true that a certain durability of tradition must obtain before legend can flourish, and tradition in most primitive societies is tenuous.) [40] For our purposes this division is not of much use. In the first place the sense of the pastness of the mythological past seems to be sometimes so vague that another way of describing the emotion involved must be found. The Eskimos have a relatively flourishing mythology; but they have practically no sense of the remote past. To the Eskimo, writes Professor Boas, "the world has always been as it is now." [41] To primitive man the mythological past is an emotion felt and not an epoch conceived. The savage's sense of pastness is closely akin to his general sense of the preternatural world. That the "mythological age" may be something personally experienced, something to which in myth-making one may "regress," is suggested by Lévy-Bruhl, who shows that certain primitive peoples use the same word to signify both "dream" and "the mythical period." If the sense of the past differs qualitatively from the general sense of the preternatural, it is perhaps because it arises from a regression to childhood. But as the psychoanalysts have shown, aesthetic activity is in many complicated ways a matter of regression to one's childhood. In this sense, "the past" surely weaves a complex pattern into all kinds of primitive literature, and it would be highly arbitrary to identify as myths those stories which explicitly refer to the past in such a way that it may be historically conceived.

Furthermore, creatures who seem to belong to "the mythical period" are always appearing in "folk tales." [42] Again, the same tale may be told of the mythological age as is told elsewhere of the present or recent past. It is of course instructive that so many peoples identify their myths as such because they are stories which take place in the mythological age, when the world was different. But we cannot be satisfied with this as a definition. If we accept it as Boas does, we do not find it of much use, nor does Boas, as is demonstrated by his most definitive essay on myth, "Folktales of the North

American Indians." Why does the mythmaker as he relates his tale to his audience imagine a time when the world was different? What use does he make of this idea? What needs call it into existence? What emotions does the evocation of the past arouse? These are questions which ask, "What is the function of myth?" And it is the *function* of myth that we must consider in answering all such questions.

Nor do other familiar distinctions between kinds of primitive literature seem ultimately fruitful. For example, the same tale may in different guises be explanatory or nonexplanatory, celestial or terrestrial; and the same tale may vary widely between the natural and the preternatural, or place a widely varying emphasis on the human, animal, spiritual, ghostly, or divine characters.[43] As Professor Boas himself remarks, when a single cultural area, such as the Northwest Coast of America, is subjected to careful analysis, it appears that the folk tales and myths constantly blend into each other.[44] It seems to me that any rigid attempt to distinguish among myth and legend and folk tale is open to so many objections as to be of very limited (though sometimes of very real) utility. What is important is to arrive at a definition of myth which cuts across these uncertain categories. First, however, let us look briefly at three theories of the historical relation between the different kinds of primitive literature.

(1) The Grimm brothers adhered to the degeneration theory which went hand in hand with Indo-European linguistics. The *Märchen* or folk tales were supposed to be remnants of primordial Aryan myths depicting "the mysterious and terrible forces of nature." They were fictitious misreadings of "a belief dating back to the most ancient times" which "can only be discovered by the most far-seeing eye." So Wilhelm Grimm wrote in 1856, three years before he died. But he seems to have had some doubts even as he wrote. He had thought that the *Märchen* "were coterminous with . . . the great race which is commonly called Indo-Germanic"—but "we see with amazement" that similar stories appear among the African Negroes and the American Indians.[45] In an earlier time Sir Walter Scott espoused the degeneration theory: "the mythology of one period," he writes, "would appear to pass into the romance of the

next, and that into the nursery tales of subsequent ages." [46] At a later time Max Müller repeated this argument. [47]

(2) In his later years, Andrew Lang became more and more interested in the folk tale, and the philosophical savage with his scientific myths began to assume a new perspective. Lang did not live to develop a full theory, but his evolutionary habit of mind led him to think that the folk tale, undoubtedly a universal phenomenon, must be anterior to the myth. "Märchen," he wrote, are the "oldest extant form of the higher myths." By "higher myth," he seems to mean legends: thus the stories of Perseus, Odysseus, Jason, Leminkainen, Maui (the Maori culture hero) are composed of earlier *Märchen*, originally told of anonymous people or animals, later localized and attached to a real or imaginary personage. He does not definitely include the myth proper—the "explanatory myth"—in this evolutionary process, contenting himself with a vague but very suggestive reference to "elaborate myths" developed by "poets and priests . . . out of the original savage data." [48] E. S. Hartland, one of Lang's colleagues in the Folklore Society, appears to have given the folk tale general primacy: "modern European folktales," he wrote, "cannot be the worn-down relics of the classical mythology. They are rather stuff of the kind out of which the classical or other mythologies grew." [49] Wilhelm Wundt says that the *Märchen* was "the original narrative," "the most permanent of all forms of literary composition." He believes that it was a product of a universal "totemic age," and even insists on what is undoubtedly true: that the content, at least, of cosmogonic myths corresponds to "Märchen of a very primitive type," though their form and import belong to a much higher stage of development. [50]

(3) The generally accepted view today is that, aside from probable but undemonstrable evolutionary theories, the folk tale is psychologically and functionally primary to the more ambitious and serious mythological tales. The tendency is to suppose that obviously philosophical or explanatory myths are tales which have been remodeled and intellectualized by gifted priests or raconteurs. No modern anthropologist would deny, however, that some highly developed myths have in some places been retold and misread in folktale style, and in this sense have degenerated.

With few exceptions, modern anthropologists agree that primitive man, like civilized man, lives in two worlds, the matter-of-fact workaday world and the magico-religious world and that he employs various psychic and social devices for keeping them separate. Primitive man is sometimes rational and practical, sometimes irrational and superstitious. He has two principles of causation: the natural and what may be rather vaguely called the supernatural.

But here a note of definition upon which much of our later argument depends. Whatever may be true of the study of religion, in the study of myth the word "preternatural" has certain advantages over the more common "supernatural." *Super*natural implies a philosophical distinction between the objective and the supersensuous which the savage does not make and which we ought not to make in studying mythopoeic psychology. Furthermore, it has misleading theological overtones. "Preternatural" means, in these pages, *that which is magical, the Uncanny, the Wonderful, the Mysterious, the Powerful, the Terrible, the Dangerous, the Extraordinary. In short, anything that has* mana *is preternatural.*

Whether or not primitive religion may best be understood by assuming a supernatural world of causes and events as opposed to a natural world, such a dualism appears to be misleading in the study of myth. The preternatural, which is aesthetically apprehended and controlled by myths, does, it is true, set itself off from the real world as we ordinarily perceive it. But that is not because it is *less* than ordinarily real but because it is far *more* than ordinarily real—an idea we shall now try to develop.

Otfried Müller's definition of myth as a narrative which unites the real and the ideal (i.e., the imaginary, not the moral ideal) is basically correct. We prefer to say, however, that myth is literature which suffuses the natural with preternatural efficacy (*mana*). But not all literature which does this is myth. Within our broad definition a myth is to be distinguished from other kinds of literature *by its function.*

In his "Myth in Primitive Psychology" Malinowski had made an admirable statement of the use of myth among the Trobriand Islanders. That mythmaking is not merely a useless and unaccountable pastime or the indulgence of one's curiosity is agreed upon by all modern anthropologists. Malinowski's statement of the functionalism of myth, however, is the most complete and perhaps the most extreme that has been made. He thinks that myth "is a hard-working, extremely important cultural force." It is "a narrative resurrection of a primeval reality, told in satisfaction of deep religious wants, moral craving, social submissions, even practical requirements." It is a pragmatic charter of primitive faith and moral wisdom which "comes into play when rite, ceremony, or a social or moral rule demands justification, warrant of antiquity, reality and sanctity." Finally, it is "a statement of primeval, greater, and more relevant reality by which the present life, fates, and activities of mankind are determined." Although he shows that myth is a strong preservative of tradition, Malinowski denies that it is dogma. It may have the efficacy of dogma, but it is at the same time plastic and dynamic. Myths are made *ad hoc,* he writes; they are "constantly regenerated; every historical change creates its mythology."

If a narrative suffuses the natural with the preternatural in reinforcement of the sanctity, the reality, the worth-whileness of any serious cultural activity of or life itself, may we not say that the narrative is a myth?

Malinowski's account of myth as we have sketched it is confined to the myth proper and does not include the folk tale. According to this account, moreover, the function of myth is primarily moral and social, rather than psychological. Any complete statement of the function of myth would have to bring out more clearly its psychological function and would have to deal with the folk tale rather than dismiss it, as does Malinowski, because it is not "serious."

Much of the time the savage, like everyone else, languishes in apathy and mechanical routine; his emotions, as Dewey writes, are often "sodden." [51] Yet he is perhaps more often capable of a dynamic and precise attention than we are. Goldenweiser writes that primitive culture is "dynamic and vibrant." [52] The tenuousness of the savage's sense of history and tradition is partly compensated for by an exaggerated system of ritual and taboos designed in part to preserve accepted values. Yet his inadequate sense of the past demands a correspondingly rich sense of the present; and his struggles in a precarious economic and a hostile natural environment make a "vibrant" sense of present reality a vital necessity. What is "real" to the savage does not, of course, mean that which is scientifically verifiable. Reality to him (to most of us, for that matter) is that which seems to have power, that which seems to have *mana*. While the need for a sense of reality may not be so pressing to those who live in a complex society which furnishes various kinds of contrived security, to the savage it is often a matter of life and death. When he is thinking and feeling at the height of his powers, he lives, as Radin says, "in a blaze of reality." [53]

If, then, the myth as distinguished from the legend and the folk tale is "a narrative resurrection of a primeval reality," we may perhaps say that myth in general is a resurrection of reality, and that, no less than the serious myths, the folk tale, which constitutes the fundamental corpus of mythology, resurrects the sense of reality by suffusing the objective universe with preternatural force—does so, that is, when it becomes mythical. Marett suggested that myth "need be no more than a sort of animatism grown picturesque." [54] We may translate this by saying that myth is *mana* grown picturesque. The psychological function of countless narratives about ghosts, magical objects, enchanted forests, lost children, malevolent, benign, or irresponsible culture heroes, animals which change into men or become their guardian spirits, cosmological beings, etc., is to fuse the perception of magical power with the perception of color, size, shape, sound, or motion.

"The world of myth," as Professor Ernst Cassirer writes, "is a dramatic world—the world of actions, of forces, of conflicting powers." [55] Now when forces are apprehended as felt qualities they become usable in an art form. But it is not only such qualities as color or sound which to the mythmaker are indistinguishable from the object which excites him. He perceives objects "physiognomically," as Cassirer says; objects change "their usual faces" in accordance with the mythmaker's emotions. Dramatic qualities in naïve experience, according to Dewey, "stand in themselves on precisely the same level as colors, sounds, qualities of contact, taste and smell. . . . Empirically things are poignant, tragic, beautiful, humorous, settled, disturbed, comfortable, annoying, barren, harsh, consoling, splendid, fearful; are such immediately in their own right and in their own behalf." [56] The magician unconsciously assumes the fusion of power, quality, and object. But besides being a compulsive technique magic is in and of itself an aesthetic activity.[57] Magic is immediately available to art, and art to magic. Myths may be regarded, on the one hand, as the aesthetic exercise which preserves and reaffirms the magic fusion; myths keep the magician's world—and the poet's world—from falling apart.[58] On the other hand, myths are poetic dramatizations of the conflicts and interactions of powers operating within the qualities and objects with which these powers seem to be identical. If these observations are sound, any narrative or poem which reaffirms the dynamism and vibrancy of the world, which fortifies the ego with the impression that there is a magically potent brilliancy or dramatic force in the world, may be called a myth.[59]

Primitive literature may also be said to perform what I venture to call the Promethean task of reconciling the conflicting forces of magic and religion. This idea, however, demands some preliminary remarks.

In his *Natural History of Religion* Hume very cannily chose examples of what we should now call magic to illustrate the myth-making mind at work. Magic is not conducive to a highly developed mythology because it does not of itself postulate spirits or gods or personifications of natural objects and forces. Nevertheless the whole groundwork of myth is magical; for the storyteller can compose myths about wonderfully potent animals and men who defy the laws of time and space, as well as the laws which limit the mutability of species, and still remain close to the confines of the psychology of magic. Magic, of course, emphasizes the power of men as opposed to the power of gods, and what interested Hume, and Herbert Spencer, was precisely the limitations which men place upon their gods. Even in highly developed mythologies we find the attitude of the magician. There are countless stories not only of the positive compulsion of gods but of gods being beaten, cajoled, bribed, tricked, scolded, and insulted.[60] This treatment of the gods is but one aspect of the pervasive desire of the storyteller to reduce divinity to human and animal stature—a desire which is entirely in accordance with the world view of the magician. Santayana, we can see, has put it rightly when he observes that "the first function of mythology is to justify magic." [61]

The system of taboo also has its influence on myth. Taboo, which may be described as "negative magic," is a social and psychological device for preserving the separation between the matter-of-fact world and the preternatural world. An object or a being which has *mana* is regarded as dangerous if it is not treated with the proper magical technique and so it is set apart—"insulated," as Marett says—from the ordinary world and its techniques.[62] A number of myths dramatize this isolation of the preternatural by reasserting its importance: myths which tell of the breaking of a taboo—such as those of Orpheus and Eurydice, Cupid and Psyche, or Lot's wife—are examples.

The question of the relation between myth and religion is a difficult one. If the reader has sometimes gained the impression that this book is a study of religion as much as of myth, that is partly due to the bias of the available literature. The missionaries who first wrote about primitive society were naturally interested primarily in religion, and so were the philosophers who studied their reports. Even the books by modern anthropologists which we have consulted for information about myth have been in many cases treatises on religion rather than on myth. This all gives the impression that religion and myth in primitive society amount to about the same thing. There is no doubt, however, that a great many myths are clearly extraneous to religion. These may be political or economic myths—stories of genealogy and social tradition which lend credence or support to a political caste or an economic system.[63] Or they may be—like some of the cosmological and cosmogonic myths of the Polynesians—creations of philosophically-minded individuals whose imagination liberates itself from the system of ritual and ceremony which for their fellows is inviolable and which constitutes the religion of the society.[64] Some students of myth, such as Hume and Lang, say that there is a deep-seated enmity between myth and religion and that the great body of popular mythology is antireligious. If we define religion as moral theism, this is undoubtedly true. The idea that there is an enmity between myth and religion contains a large element of truth, as we shall see, even if, with Tylor, we define religion as "the belief in spiritual beings." If, on the other hand, we mean by religion the whole magico-religious complex, then we may say that the great majority of myths are religion in literary form. We should not, however, confuse religion with theology.

Theology and theological dogma have always been the preoccupation of a very limited number of men; and a purely theological myth is an impossibility.

The influence of exceptional individuals upon myth has come to seem more and more important in recent decades; and a full study of these individuals and their relations with the mass of men would doubtless help us to find our way about in the bewildering variety of mythology. We can at least glance at this question briefly. Professor Boas writes that "the parallelism of distribution of religious or social groups led by single individuals and of complex mythologies is so striking that there can be little doubt in regard to their psychological connection. The Mexicans, the Pueblo tribes, the Pawnee, the Bella Coola, the Maidu may be given as examples. The contrast between a disorganized mass of folktales and the more systematic mythologies seems to lie, therefore, in the introduction of an element of *individual* creativeness in the latter. The priest or chief as a poet or thinker takes hold of the folk traditions and of isolated rituals and elaborates them in dramatic or poetic form. Their systematization is brought about by the centralization of thought in one mind." [65] Here again we are at the mercy of the available literature. The individuals whom anthropologists have studied are primarily religious leaders, and we cannot say definitely to what extent the religious leader is the creator of myths, or to what extent the creator of myths is religious. Important questions such as the temperament and social position and function of the primitive literary man (in so far as he is identifiable as such) must go unanswered until a study is made of him. Like the poets and critics of the late eighteenth century we would like to know more about the primitive bard. The religious leader, however, must have exerted a powerful influence either directly or indirectly on the making of myths; and we do know something of him.

According to Paul Radin, the religious leader is motivated by two complementary desires: to consolidate his position as a member of an economically privileged caste and to satisfy his craving as an intellectual for order, objectivity, and form. His task is "to interpret and manipulate the psychological correlates of the economic-social realities." [66] The priest-thinker is of course generally in favor of religion rather than magic, and his lifework is devoted to displacing or reinterpreting magic—in other words, to divesting the individual of the prerogative he gains from magic and to transferring power from man to the gods. Thus his purpose is to establish a belief in spiritual beings who have objective reality and exist independently of magical practices; for, to the ordinary man, spirits and gods, if they exist at all, seem to do so only when they produce desired effects, and even then they are far from clearly conceived. The priest's task is to transfer the emotions attached to magic technique and belief to religion.[67] To this end he creates independent, powerful gods, and, as Radin says, establishes a variety of spirits and deities who retain many of the qualities of the magical imagination and who are still close to the "life-values" of man. These spirits and deities, a kind of compromise between magic and religion, are the stock in trade of mythmakers; the tensions aroused and the reconciliations effected between the religious desire for an omnipotent deity and the general human preference for powerful anthropomorphic and theriomorphic beings are universally stamped upon mythology. We feel something of this tension, for example, in the wars of the Titans against God or, as in Grimm's *Fairy Tales*, the battle of man and his friendly animals against the devilish monsters. Radin has found traces of the different stages of this struggle in Winnebago myth. In one myth the young buffalo spirits in heaven are warned not to smell the smoke of tobacco offerings rising from the earth because if they do they will be doomed to descend to earth as real buffaloes and be shot. Here the magical prerogative remains; the spirits are partly in the power of man. Other myths place man in a more abject position. Thus Earthmaker, the supreme, or at least superior, god of the Winnebagos is said to have given all of his gifts to the spirits (just as Epimetheus gives all of *his* to the animals) so that he had none left for man, whom he created last. Therefore he condescends to grant the requests of man if they are correctly made. In myths which are still more religious the spirits are openly contemptuous of man and plague him by sending spurious messengers to suppliants, or man is portrayed in complete abjection before the gods.

Psychologically we may state the difference between magic and religion thus: magic is the envelopment and coercion of the objective world by the ego; it is a dynamic subjectivism. Religion is the coercion of the ego by gods and spirits who are objectively conceived beings in control of nature and man.[68] This fundamental clash of emotions and attitudes must be felt pervasively, if unconsciously, in primitive society (the terms we have used could probably be translated so as to apply to civilized society as well as primitive). I suggest that myth dramatizes in poetic form the disharmonies, the deep neurotic disturbances which may be occasioned by this clash of inward and outward forces, and that by reconciling the opposing forces, by making them interact coercively toward a common end, myth performs a profoundly beneficial and life-giving act. This I call the Promethean function of myth. For Prometheus is the intermediary between God and man. He is the dynamic principle and art of life, and he helps man to defend himself against the old Zeus, who treacherously seeks, as Toynbee writes, to set "his foot on the neck of a prostrate Universe." It is the destiny of Zeus to grow remote, tyrannical, frozen, inhuman, and reactionary. It is the destiny of man to rebel against this tyranny. Prometheus resolves the struggle in favor of man and shows him how to use the energies called forth by his war against Zeus.

3.

There can be no doubt that the psychic peculiarities of the religious leader have left an indelible impression on myth. This is most noteworthy among peoples who exalt the shaman type of leader. The shaman is distinguished from his fellows by being deeply neurotic and sometimes epileptic. He is capable of the utmost extremes of depression and mania and of enduring great hardships in self-imposed isolation, through which he attains, in the eyes of his tribe, a supernatural sanction. As an initiate of the shaman caste he may retire to a lonely hut where he subjects himself to the greatest rigors of discomfort and starvation; he has trances; and he emerges from his ordeal having attained, as Radin says, "a new normalcy and reintegration." Radin suggests that the many myths concerning the change of seasons, the death and rebirth of nature (of which Frazer makes so much in *The Golden Bough*), are primarily accounts of the psychic ordeal of the religious neurotic and only secondarily nature myths. Is not this psychic ordeal a profoundly human phenomenon which we ought to consider when thinking of a great variety of mythical themes? To name a few—awakening after a deep, deathlike sleep, the folk heroes who are beheaded and magically restored, the death and rebirth of the savior-gods (Christ, Attis, Adonis, Osiris, etc.), the retirement of youths at puberty, the banishment and return of heroes such as Oedipus, the ordeal of the Arthurian heroes in their search for the Grail, the theme of "withdrawal-and-return" on which Toynbee has based his *Study of History*. These mythical themes have in common the withdrawal of the ego from the objective world and the subsequent return of the ego transfigured and possessed of a new potency. In some primitive societies at least, the shaman embodied this rhythm of the psyche. Radin says that after the shaman's ordeal, he was accepted by his fellows as a superhuman being who could change into an animal, travel at will through time and space, go to the spirit world, or be possessed by a spirit. In other words, he could do what the characters of all mythical tales can do. Some myths, then, may in one sense be considered biographies of the shaman's psychic ordeal. But the shaman's life only gave dramatic form—suitable to literature—to those fundamental rhythms which all men feel: waking and sleeping, life and death, day and night, fruition and decay, stability and instability, dispersal and consolidation. These psychobiological rhythms and operations of the universe "resound," as Dewey might say, in the tones, sensations, and metaphors of myth— an insight which led both Vico and Tylor to hold that myth was prelinguistic. Myth is immanent in all living organisms—in what Herder calls "the evolution, the enduring, and the annihilations."

We might observe at this point that the value of euhemerism is its emphasis on the humanness of mythology. The magical or terrible beasts, the witches and sorcerers, the tricksy or noble heroes of mythology should not be described as "faded gods," as they have sometimes been called; rather are the gods faded beasts, magicians, and heroes. Stated thus negatively, euhemerism is profoundly true. As a positive doctrine to the effect that gods are only apotheosized individual men, it is at best extremely narrow. Spirits, magical forces, natural phenomena are potential gods just as much as heroic or remarkable men. Yet some divine heroes and some deities are nevertheless deified men. This is naturally impossible to prove by reference to very many specific deified men, since primitive peoples are notoriously lacking in historians. But when we learn from Pausanias [69] that the heroes of Marathon were worshiped down to the second century A.D., or that among European rustics, as in *Finnegans Wake*, Napoleon and Wellington became figures "in a mummers' drama of the seasons," [70] we seem to have tangible proof.

The Library of Apollodorus lays great stress on Greek genealogical stories and heroic legends and consequently lends credibility to Frazer's observation (in his preface to *The Library*) that "many, perhaps most, of the legendary persons" in Apollodorus "were men of flesh and blood, the memory of whose fortunes and family relationships survived in oral tradition until they were embalmed in Greek literature." In Frazer's opinion, euhemerism "contains a substantial element of truth." [71] Though euhemerism is hard to test as a general theory, we can at least briefly examine some of the conditions of primitive society which make it plausible.

Ancestor worship or the worship of the ghosts of the dead in general lends support to the theory of Euhemerus; this, as we have seen, was Spencer's reason for embracing the theory. Later writers have shown, however, that clearly discernible ancestor worship is by no means a universal custom and that it is nonexistent among the most primitive tribes. [72] It is found, nevertheless, in West Africa, Melanesia, and of course in China and Japan; [73] and we may doubtless conclude that in these places men have become spirits and gods.

Paul Radin is inclined to find more truth in Spencer's doctrine of ghosts than do most contemporary anthropologists: "the dead and the ghosts of the dead were the materials out of which the notion of spirits actually developed. . . . Religion itself, in contrast to magic, can very well be regarded as having been originally differentiated from magic, and subsequently fostered, by this extension to the dead of all the attitudes and types of intercourse and behavior that had been characteristic of the living." The economic and social condition of primitive society is sometimes conducive to the apotheosis of human beings. In the simplest cultures, Radin says, there is an intense struggle among the priests for power. In more complex cultures, this very human struggle is apotheosized into a struggle among spirits who compete for man's favor or for power over him. Among the Eskimo the deities who represent natural phenomena are all supposed to have once been men: "the hardness and cruelty of their relation to human beings reflect this origin." This is of course to the advantage of the shamans, and needless to say, the deities are not cruel to them.[74] Besides the economic reason for making gods out of men, there is a strong psychological reason; which is that according to the magical world view such phenomena as disease and death are supposed to be the work of hostile sorcerers, or if hostile spirits are imagined, their evil machinations are supposed to be carried out through the agency of a sorcerer—since the practice of magic requires a *human* coercer.[75]

We should expect euhemerism to gain new stature from the modern interest in exceptional individual savages. Thus Boas writes that the culture-hero myths, which are of great importance in American Indian mythologies, probably originated in "an interesting story told of some personage" and "the striking and important exploits ascribed to him." [76] And Radin is willing to say that "man created spirits and deities originally in the image of the shaman." [77] Radin, however, hastens to disclaim the title of euhemerist.

Certain ritual and political practices make it seem probable that savages thought men could become gods. In the Zuñi cult of the masked gods "a man, when he puts on the mask of the god, becomes for the time being the supernatural himself. He has no longer human speech, but only the cry which is peculiar to that god." [78] Frazer's *Golden Bough* is full of divine human beings: Semiramis, Frazer writes, seems to have been both Astarte and a real woman or "series of real women, whether queens or harlots, whose memory survives in ancient history." In the Middle East a human couple annually acted out the roles of "the loving goddess and the dying god": e.g., Aphrodite and Adonis, Cybele and Attis, Isis and Osiris. Of divine kings there were also plenty.[79] Finally, Freud has lent support to the theory of euhemerism by supposing with a large measure of justification that God is one's own father or mother.

Euhemerism cannot be accepted as a generally true doctrine. But it will always seem profoundly suggestive to those who perceive that the gods are not revealed from on high but have to be made painfully out of human stuff and at an untold cost of suffering and confusion, or perhaps sometimes gods are made out of men in the spirit of a jest or a satire.

CHAPTER VII

MYTH AND PSYCHOANALYSIS

So FAR our method has been akin to the method of pragmatic naturalism. We have found ample support among those who have advanced formal descriptions of myth for Andrew Lang's statement that the history of mythological studies "is the history of rash, premature, and exclusive theories"; and we have consequently given up formal description and have tried to identify certain kinds of aesthetic experience as mythical. Myth is experience no less than art. And we can best study "experience" by studying the interactions of human emotions with the environment of men. It seems to me that we can learn more about myth in this way than in any other.

Yet pragmatism loses something by directing its attention outward into the present environment, for in doing so it makes the human organism too malleable and the emotions too adaptable. It obscures the sense of one's own past; it is too forward-looking, perhaps too optimistic, for it ignores the very human feeling of fate and the sense of the inexorable tragedy of having been born a human being. Every pragmatist should be pursued now and then by the Eumenides.

I venture to think that the psychoanalyst's belief in the rigidity and desperation of the instincts is misguided and that the pragmatist is ultimately right when he says that men are motivated by more plastic and controllable agencies. Nevertheless, the belief in these somber death and sex drives deepens and enriches our understanding of human nature beyond the depth and richness which pragmatism offers. Whether or not the instincts exist, they make a "powerful melody" [1] in the writings of Freud. In a study of myth we should be misguided if we ignored psychoanalysis. And I refer primarily to Freud's psychoanalysis. I agree with Freud's somewhat humorless estimate of himself: He *was* the best psychoanalyst.

2.

First we must consider Freud as an anthropologist. Freud of course equates the psychic development of the individual with the psychic development of the race. He is not by any means the first to do this. "The childhood of humanity" is a phrase which perhaps all of the pre-twentieth-century students of myth accepted as a description of primitive times. Freud is only repeating a traditional idea in his own terms when he tells us that the primitive world view of magic and animatism corresponds with the narcissistic fantasies of early childhood. Both are subjective; both assume that the inward emotions are the only reality. According to Freud, religion, which replaces magic and is the second stage of human thought, corresponds with the libidinous object-finding of the maturing child, as he learns to displace his sexual drives from himself to his parents. The third and final stage of cultural evolution is the scientific, and this corresponds to the individual's acceptance of objective reality and his subordination of the pleasure principle, which may be loosely described as the unrestricted exercise of wish-fulfilling fantasies, usually sexual. The individual finally realizes, in other words, that the pleasure principle is "useless" and "dangerous" to the organism and that he must accept "the reality principle." [2]

Now since each of us as a child lives through a primitive age (so runs the psychoanalyst's argument) and since we are never able to abandon our childish fancies completely but can only repress them more or less successfully into our unconscious, we retain in the depths of our minds certain survivals. These survivals appear most readily in our dreams. Freud says that dreams are "acts of regression"; they "preserve . . . psychical antiquities"; [3] when we dream we think like savages. The neurotic and the artist, according to this theory, revert to primitive thought most readily. [4]

The emotional complex which dreams, neurosis, and artistic creation reinstate in the mind Freud believes (or seems to believe) to have arisen from a historical event which took place in primeval times. This was the killing and eating of the primeval father by his sons. The instinctual emotions which led to this primeval parricide and the feelings of guilt aroused by it are called, of course, the Oedipus complex, and this is "the central complex of the neuroses in general." [5] The savage emotions and guilt feelings forged in the fury of the parricide have been molded into our artistic, religious, and social culture; and culture has in turn been conditioned by this particular complex of emotions. As Ariel says, there is nothing of the father

> that doth fade
> But doth suffer a sea-change
> Into something rich and strange.[6]

How does all this appear to the anthropologists? We have already on several occasions pointed out the mistake of assuming that all primitive thought is childish fantasy. We have also shown that over-all theories of cultural evolution are nearly always more misleading than a skeptical, or even antievolutionary, attitude. The anthropologists were quick to dispose of Freud's theories on these and other grounds. They were too quick, as is shown by a glance at Goldenweiser's nonsensical statement (1922) that "Totem and Taboo" is "without any foundation whatsoever in the known facts of history or biology," [7] an idea which is immediately refuted by a little introspection, as well as by a mountain of facts.

More sober reflection has partially reinstated Freud's theory. A. L. Kroeber gives what seems to be the general opinion among anthropologists.[8] According to Kroeber, we cannot accept Freud's account of historical evolution nor his account of the genesis and function of totems, taboos, magic, and religion. Yet Freud's thesis is true if we mean by it that "certain psychic processes tend always to be operative and to find expression in widespread human institutions. Among these processes would be the incest drive and incest repression, filial ambivalence and the like; in short, if one like, the kernel of the Oedipus situation." [9] Malinowski, in his *Sex and Repression in Savage Society*, tests Freud's thesis as it applies to a matrilineal culture, precisely where we should expect to find it inapplicable. He concludes that in a matrilineal culture the Oedipus complex is modified but still present.[10] "Freud's theories not only roughly correspond to human psychology . . . they follow closely

the modifications in human nature brought about by various con-
stitutions of society." [11] Thus the familiar complaint that the
Oedipus complex is confined to the European *bourgeoisie* of the
twentieth century is mistaken—though it is undoubtedly true that
what different cultures do to accentuate or to guard against the
Oedipus complex is as important as the existence of the complex
itself.

Freud did not prove, of course, that all savages are neurotics; it
is questionable whether he meant to. All he says is that there are
"numerous points of correspondence" between the "psychology
. . . of folklore" and "the psychology of the neurotic," [12] as there
undoubtedly are. There can be no doubt, for example, of the correspondence between magic and compulsive neurosis, for both depend on the overvaluation of psychic phenomena as opposed to
objective reality and on the belief that certain manipulative ex-
ercises can control the universe. To the student of myth the important general conclusion of psychoanalysis is that the artist and
the neurotic and the dreamer have much in common both with one
another and with the primitive magico-mythical psychology.

3.

Herder thought that myths were much like dreams, and Tylor
wrote that the dreams of primitive peoples had exercised a great
influence on myth—because the savage saw his own form, or someone else's, in dreams and deduced the idea of spirits from these
apparitions which functioned independently of their bodies.[13] But
Tylor did not study the psychology of dreams very intently. If, as
Ernest Jones believes, psychoanalysis furnishes "the key to mythology," it does so largely by its interpretation of dreams.[14] Let us
note certain preliminary relationships between dreams and myths.

We should expect certain basic biological and social similarities
to produce similar dreams among all peoples of the world. This
seems to be borne out by J. S. Lincoln in his *The Dream in Primitive
Culture*.[15] Lincoln writes that the same processes of wish fulfillment,
conflict between the censor and the dream thoughts, symbolization,
displacement, condensation, and secondary elaboration [16] create the
dreams of all peoples. He maintains that all of Freud's symbols—for

father, mother, birth, death, sexual organs, etc.—occur in primitive dreams as well as civilized. We may safely assume, at least, that psychologically the dreams of savages are not different from our own.

We cannot assume, however, that dreams and myths are indistinguishable, as do such psychoanalysts as Rank, Abraham, and Jung.[17] Freud usually seems to assume that there is little difference between dreams and myths: they are both, he thinks, disguised fulfillments of suppressed wishes. But this is far more true of dreams than of myths, though we shall have occasion to notice later that myths may sometimes be wish fulfillments.

The psychoanalysts conceive of myths as collections or systems of symbols; but though the analyst may find some utility in thinking of them as such, myths are not primarily symbolic. According to Freud, furthermore, dreams are asocial, and largely though not entirely unconscious. But like all literature, myth makes moral responses to society and is created under the guidance of the conscious intellect.

Again according to Freud (the classic Freud as opposed to the Freud of *Beyond the Pleasure Principle*), dreams are the expression of the pleasure principle; they afford the dreamer a way out of having to face reality; they are hedonistic fantasy and as such would (presumably) be of no use to anyone who succeeded in effecting a complete adjustment to the reality principle. Now myth, as we have seen, is much more than an escape into pleasurable fantasy. Far from it, it is a "resurrection of reality." Here we meet with that ostensible underestimation of poetry and myth as nothing but infantile fantasy which has led so many people to suppose that Freud was anticultural, or at least that he had no understanding of poetry. But this judgment comes from seizing upon Freud's explicit statements about poetry, which are usually mistaken, and ignoring his implicit understanding of poetry, which was profound.

In the rest of this chapter I shall try to do two things: show how psychoanalysis reasserts certain reactionary ideas about myth which we have already met in early parts of the book and show how psychoanalysis can help us to a firmer understanding of literature as myth than we have so far achieved.

4.

Much of the study of myth by the psychoanalysts has been no more than a remodeling of the Max Müller kind of investigation to fit the psychoanalytic theory. In Abraham's *Dreams and Myths* we are told that Adalbert Kuhn is "the founder of comparative mythology." If the Aryan scholars tell us that primitive men thought only in the metaphors of a sublime natural philosophy, Abraham tells us that their thinking consisted of symbolic sexual fantasies. If to the Aryan scholars, the sun was the supreme natural and therefore mythological phenomenon, to Abraham the sun is "the fire of life," i.e., the libido. Ernest Jones, too, is unduly influenced by, if not committed to, the Aryan nature mythologists.[18] For Jung, "mythology" is usually associated with the Aryanism, Buddhism, Mithraism, or the sun theories of Frobenius.[19] Rank tells us naïvely that the Aryan theory of Vedic origins is outmoded and has been replaced by the Babylonian school.[20] Thus in his *Myth of the Birth of the Hero* he takes Sargon to be the prototype of mythological heroes such as Moses, Oedipus, Tristan, Romulus, Jesus, and Osiris. The psychoanalysts make the salutary suggestion that mythology is not primarily concerned with natural phenomena but with human nature, i.e., mostly man's sexuality. But since they adopt the irrational method of going to the nature mythologists, instead of to the anthropologists, to prove this, their theories are burdened with philological error.

As we might expect, the psychoanalysts use some of the etymological devices discussed in our section on Max Müller. There is no doubt that unconscious etymologies and puns do contribute to the formation of dreams. Freud pointed out that part of the apparent absurdity of dreams can be explained by supposing that unconscious "dream thoughts" may be expressed by the dreamer in a single word or figure of speech which in turn is made into a visual image.[21] Thus in the dream of one of Freud's patients, concerning the Wagnerian opera that went on and on until 7:45 A.M., the idea that a certain man "towered over" his fellows was precipitated into an image of this man in the form of the conductor, who led the orchestra from atop a tower. This is the same process which the philologists imputed to the mythmaker. First they supposed primeval man to have had sublime thoughts about the universe. These thoughts were expressed in metaphors; and the metaphors were later used by myth-makers who were less intelligent than the primeval philosophers or who had simply forgotten the original language (e.g., exchanged "Aryan" for Greek); these mythmakers took the metaphors at their face value, as statements of fact rather than as metaphors, and this accounts for the apparent absurdity of myths. The psychoanalysts have therefore resuscitated the old theory of the "poverty" of primitive language, which we first met in Vico and Heyne. This theory holds that the primitive man's thoughts were too sublime or complicated to be expressed by his language except by the distortion of figurative speech—just as the psychoanalysts believe that the devices open to the dreamer are incommensurable with the dream thoughts and consequently distort them. But this is obviously much easier to demonstrate in dreams than in myths. In a clinical analysis of the dreamer, we may be able to recover the original thoughts by free association. The Aryan, or other "original philosophy," can be recovered only by the most untrustworthy conjecture.

The psychoanalyst supposes, as Abraham says, that "the majority of myths are presented in a symbolic manner and so in reality they must contain something or mean something that their outer form does not signify." [22] This is based on the theory that dreams must be considered as existing on two levels: "the latent" and "the manifest." By analogy myths are supposed also to have a latent content and a manifest content. This idea—that myths seem to be one thing but are really something else—was held in one way or another by almost all the older students of myth, from the Stoics down to Vico, Herder, Creuzer, the Vedic scholars, and even Tylor and Lang. But whether we consider the latent content to consist of natural philosophy or of sex wishes, the theory is misleading. It is useful in studying dreams, but when the psychoanalysts (or anyone else!) apply it to myths it becomes dangerously seductive. The psychoanalysts turn from dreams to myths with a preconceived idea about sexual symbolism; they simply translate this idea into the latent content of myths and then interpret the myths as if they were nothing but veils drawn over a "real" meaning. Most American anthropologists agree that myths are not disguised sexual symbolism—or indeed symbolism of any sort.[23] They are just what they seem to be.

We shall have to look in other directions for light from psychoanalysis on the study of myth.

5.

Still, in spite of the fact that comparisons between dreams and myths are often precarious, certain useful comparisons can be made. In the first place dreams cannot be separated sharply from the products of the waking mind. Freud insists upon this; "many of the achievements which are a matter for wonder in a dream," he says, "are now no longer to be attributed to dreaming, but to unconscious thinking, which is active during the day." [24] It must be obvious that some of the same unconscious thinking goes into the creation of myths as goes into the creation of dreams. So far in this chapter we have followed the Freudian interpretation of dreams—according to which we are admonished not to consider the dream as a functional whole and not to regard dream images as pictures in their own right but as symbols or "hieroglyphics" to be analyzed.[25] It seems to me, however, that some dreams, at least, merit consideration as aesthetic creations of a very high order and that much might be gained by treating them as such—perhaps in the same manner as we treated myths in the last chapter.[26] Dreams are in this sense a reason for an optimistic view of human nature and a guarantee that art is indigenous and indestructible.

Once we begin to think of dreams as naïve aesthetic productions, we cannot help comparing them with myths. They certainly influence each other *as such* in primitive culture. Many anthropologists have noticed that certain motifs are shared by the dreams and myths of a given people, and have supposed that they influence and reinforce each other.[27]

The Freudian analysis of dreams has shown us how much of our energy and attention is absorbed by wishful thinking, how strong is the human penchant for fantasy. The reader may have felt before this that our explanations of myth have made myth out to be more durably functional and purposeful than it is. Is myth always engaged in social ratification or in fitting the human organism to carry on the struggle for survival, or in healing neurosis? Is not myth a seductive or voluptuous illusion, is it not a fantastic or playful palace of art? May it not isolate men from the world rather than bringing them to face it? May it not be the maternal song of earth, Circe's song, calling men back into the mud? May it not be the free play of the pleasure principle, which, rather than being healthful is simply harmless, or perhaps even, in the words of Freud, "useless and indeed extremely dangerous" to the human organism? [28] Professor Ruth Benedict, who does not accept the psychoanalytic interpretations of myth, tells us that "myth . . . is an articulate vehicle of a people's wishful thinking . . . it is universally the wishful projection of a universe of will and intention." [29] Surely this more seductive side of myth must be kept in mind when we try to grasp it in its totality. Having tried throughout this book to disburden myth of its supposed philosophical implications, we should not in turn encumber it with somber social and biological functions which do not in fact belong to it. [30] Let us remember, however, that we are not trying to give a complete account of myth but only to find out how we can study it most accurately.

We have spoken of myth as a suffusion of the natural with preternatural forces. We may now reword this idea in the following manner: myth is an aesthetic device for bringing the imaginary but powerful world of preternatural forces into a manageable collaboration with the objective facts of life in such a way as to excite a sense of reality amenable to both the unconscious passions and the conscious mind. "Reality," as I use it here, does not of course mean objective fact (which is what Freud appears to mean by "reality"), but operative, magical fact, the fact of aesthetic experience. Now if we translate this concept into the inner world of the mind, we see that dreams perform something of the same task. First, however, a glance at a somewhat fantastic but very useful terminology.

Freud's earlier conception of the unconscious and the conscious was later clarified in his book called *The Ego and the Id*.[31] According to Freud's later formulation, the ego cuts across the unconscious-conscious distinction: it is both. But the conscious part of the ego is the object-finding agent of the mind; it strives outward, against the will, as it were, of the id, and tries "to mediate" between the id and the objective world. The id is composed of all those impulses which seek to reabsorb the ego and to give the organism over to subjectivism and the pleasure principle; by means of "repression resistances" the ego keeps the impulses of the id in a state of unconsciousness.

Dreams are made by the "conflict and co-operation" [32] of two psychic forces: the "daemonic power" [33] of the id and the resisting force of the ego exercised by its deputy, the censor. We may thus think of both myths and dreams as compromises between man's daemonic impulses and objective facts—for these impulses must be controlled and used whether they are in the depths of the mind or are projected into the external world. But at this point we must broaden our conception of "objective fact." For in both myths and dreams, the ego must mediate between the id and the superego, i.e., that function of the psyche which seeks to impose the prevailing moral code upon the id. Thus the expression "objective fact" takes on a moral as well as a psychological significance.[34]

Myths and dreams, then, approach each other closely in the arena of daemonic forces. But they select different objects for representation and grow in different environments—dreams being molded among the dark organs of the body whereas myths flourish at large among the activities of men and nature. Myths make more subtle and complicated responses to morality than we find in the brutal denials and evasions of dreams; and, like all literature, myths have moral effects upon our conduct which dreams have not. Nevertheless, we see the same daemonic powers in the incandescent images of myth as we see in the more somber images of dreams. Behind the images of myth lurk the same multitude of spirits and ghosts, striving for personification, that lurk behind the dream images.

Have we not found in this brief sketch of the conflict between the id and the ego a broader formulation of the conflict between magic and religion which, following Radin, we described in the last chapter?

As we remarked above, it is very dangerous to suppose, on the analogy of dreams, that there is a latent content in every myth or every mythology. But if we look for a moment at several myths of one culture and consider them just as they appear on the surface, we are sometimes struck by what is at any rate a suggestive analogy with dreams. The latent content, according to Freud's formulation, is the mass of brutal, impulsive, or amoral dream thoughts which the ego has repressed. The manifest content is the dream as it first appears to the dreamer, after it has been subjected to a process of selection, condensation, and distortion by the censor: it is the office of the censor to prevent the painful guilt feelings which an unvarnished representation of the dream thought would occasion. The censor makes the dream respectable to the dreamer, whose idea of respectability, we must remember, is dependent upon the culture he lives in, and further, upon whatever agency is able in some measure to enforce a particular pattern on culture. Dreams have two levels; one is a kind of flux of brutality and irresponsibility and the other is a kind of stasis imposed by the prudential censor.

Now many writers have found it expedient to think of myth as existing on two levels. Vico supposed that myths contained evidence both of the nobility of the Divine Age and of the degeneracy of ensuing ages. Hume made a distinction between the moral, theistic level of myth and a lower, more amoral and animal level. Andrew Lang distinguished between the "rational" and the absurd, "irrational" levels of myth. Paul Radin has shown that the mythological beings of the Winnebagos, such as Thunderbird, Hare, and Morning Star take on different guises.[35] According to whether they appear in the popular "folkloristic" tales or in tales influenced by the shamans, they vary between the theriomorphic and the anthropomorphic, the amoral and the moral, plastic concreteness and abstraction. Do we not find here evidence of a struggle we have met before: namely the struggle between mankind in general and the priest-thinker, between the magician and the religious man? Does not the inward censor officiate in the mind of man over all aesthetic activities, as the priest-thinker officiates outwardly? Do not the censor and the priest sometimes become indistinguishable?

I do not propose to answer these difficult questions but will content myself with noticing a favorite mythological character who should be examined more closely. This is the Transformer; he appears in many, perhaps most, mythologies, but has best been studied by the American anthropologists. The Transformer is the being who changed the world as it was originally into its present condition; [36] he it was who, as Boas writes, "killed monsters that infested the land, and gave man the arts that made life worth living"; he it was who transformed the shadowy beings of the primeval world, making some into animals and others into men, and who taught men to kill animals, to make fire, and to clothe themselves.[37] Now the Transformer often appears in two guises: he may be a Promethean culture hero, a benevolent being who wishes to protect and benefit mankind, but he is much more likely to appear as a trickster (such as the Raven, Mink, Bluejay, Coyote, Old Man, Manabosho, or Glooscap of the American Indians), an irresponsible or utterly selfish creature who benefits man incidentally in pursuing his own libidinous or rapacious desires. Boas conjectures that in the original American mythologies the selfish and libidinous Transformer appeared much more undisguisedly than he does in later versions, and that he was pictured as a moral being only gradually "with the progress of society." [38] Indeed, the discrepancy in his character sometimes becomes so striking and "the friction between the two groups of tales" so pronounced, that the "personage of the Transformer [is] split in two or more parts, the one representing the true culture hero, the other retaining the features of the trickster." [39]

It is interesting to observe that Boas falls back on the idea of evolutionary progress to explain the dual character of the Transformer. He may be right in doing so. But are there not two self-interested and powerful agencies at work in the making of these myths: the censor and the priest? [40]

Many writers have thought that both religion and myth originate in the sentiment of fear. Agitated by fear, Hume says, primitive man looks upon the disordered world " with a trembling curiosity" and perceives "the first obscure traces of divinity." Later students found it necessary to broaden the primary mythical emotion so as to include awe, wonder, or the sense of the Extraordinary. Psychoanalysis furnishes us with an idea which brings a measure of clarity to the relation between the fearful or awful and myth. Rousseau seems to have grasped at a great truth when he observed that an object may make two impressions upon us, according to whether it appears familiar or unfamiliar. In an essay on "The 'Uncanny,' " Freud tells us that what we perceive as uncanny is something at once unfamiliar and yet strangely familiar.[41] A thought, an emotion, an image is "uncanny" if it appears to us suddenly and against our will out of our own past; it is, in other words, a wish long ago repressed which reappears before us. Thus a sudden and involuntary violation of the psychic order we have imposed upon ourselves produces the sensation of uncanniness. We are confronted by our own ghosts, which we had thought were safely banished. I suggest that myth is the repository of repressed wishes and that part of the magic power of myth stems from its ability to furnish "recognition scenes," in which we have the thrilling experience of coming face to face with a disinherited part of ourselves.

We may describe the uncanny as an involuntary repetition. But about repetition itself there is more to be said.

The repetitious patterns of the universe—the appearances and disappearances in nature, the dispersals and consolidations, the instabilities and stabilities—seem to romantics such as Herder and pragmatists such as James an affirmation of life. And myth, as we have hinted, may be taken as a celebration of the vitality of the universe —or at least as a preserver of life in the individual. Freud's *Beyond the Pleasure Principle* both affirms and denies this view of myth.

One cannot read many myths without being struck (and often bored) by the innumerable repetitions they contain. Thus where we are content with *one* account of how a hero approaches a monster and kills him, or attempts to, the mythmaker prefers to tell us of seven heroes who try their prowess against the monster in succession and in exactly the same way. Myths are full of such mysteriously repetitious acts. How are we to explain this?

Freud discovered in neurotic behavior, in dreams, and in the play of children what he called a "repetition compulsion." This compulsion sometimes went "beyond the pleasure principle"; i.e., not only were pleasant experiences reinstated in the imagination but also unpleasant ones. And this second kind of repetition he took to be more fundamental than the first. He believed that the repetition compulsion was a device employed by the organism to guard against psychic trauma, a device to set up a tension of modified fear—"apprehension" is the word he used—so as to prepare the psyche to meet sudden onslaughts of fright. According to Freud the mind is much better equipped to guard against stimuli from the outside world than against stimuli from within. The act of projecting inner emotions into the outer world (i.e., the first act of mythmaking) is a self-protective measure. The finished myth may perhaps be considered, as

Freud considers the painful kind of dream, a device for sending small and controllable armies of stimuli against the individual psyche as a repeated warning, so to speak, against that large army which may suddenly burst through the gates if the guard is let down. The "ghosts" of myth are indeed, as Andrew Lang said, "practically useful."

Here we discern another way in which myth fits us for life. It is instructive to remember that the eighteenth-century man, of all men the most terrified of his own unconscious, generally supposed that the emotion of fear was the pervasive primitive emotion and that it was responsible for religion. By refusing to make mythical projections of his own unconscious, he laid himself more readily open to fear than men have commonly done. In Dr. Johnson, great and manly as he was, we see the eighteenth century clutching compulsively at the inviolable Rules and trembling in horror.

Surely our argument has led us to one of the crucial problems of modern art and modern culture. We have been made, singly and in private, the trustees of inhumanly powerful forces which were once caged and domesticated by the apparatus of the Christian religion. Henry James, who in company with his father and brother was forced by temperament to confront the undisciplined terrors of his own unconscious, examined our problem with tenacious care. The ghosts which haunt certain of his characters, such as the governess in *The Turn of the Screw* and the too scrupulous gentlemen epitomized in *The Beast in the Jungle,* are terrible and destructive just because they are inadequately projected by their victims. In contrast to the mythical beings they might and should become, they remain uncreated. They remain secret and internal, appearing outwardly only in uncontrollable hallucinations which demoralize their victims, if they do not actually drive them into the grave. As Philip Rahv says, these figures of James's stories "forfeit their allotted share of experience through excessive pride or delicacy or rationality." Pride, delicacy, and rationality [42]—perhaps this is a good formulation of the scruples which keep us from mythicizing "the beast." We must do with "the beast" what James himself did: flush it from the jungle so that it may be captured in the texture of aesthetic experience and bent to our will.

In *Beyond the Pleasure Principle* Freud brings out a darker and more sinister side to the repetition compulsion. He believes that the principle of repetition is the "death instinct"—that what the organism is ultimately trying to reinstate is nothing less than the inorganic state of death. The pattern of repetition in dreams, hallucinations, children's play, in art, in the universe at large is the instinctual effort to defeat the life instincts (i.e., the sexual instincts) and bring life to rest in complete integration with the material universe. All the life instincts can do, he says, is to force the organism to take more or less devious routes and thus postpone as long as possible the inevitable victory of the impulse to die. According to this view, the pattern of compulsive repetition in the products of the human imagination represents man's dramatization of the death instinct. But these are obscure ideas, and Freud himself tells us that they are no more than hypothesis.

Freud does not speak of myth in *Beyond the Pleasure Principle*. Yet the book is important to us because here Freud explicitly says that the deeper imaginative productions of the human mind cannot be fully explained by the pleasure principle. Implicitly he has shown that myth (whether we stress the death instinct or not) has a profound function in human life. This is important because when he talks explicitly, he usually considers it as useless or harmful fantasy. Freud is not the only modern writer who teaches us much by what he does and much less by what he thinks he is doing. Sir James Frazer is another of those who give us a sense of the extraordinary wealth and complication of human emotions while themselves subscribing to a shallow scientific rationalism. There seems to be a need in our time for this sort of somnambulism.

Freud gives us certain insights into the role of intellection in dreams which we may perhaps apply with reservations to myth—more especially to the scientific theory that myths give us rational explanations of things. In the first place, he points out that the same dream content may mean different things at different times or may mean several things at one time. That this is true of myths has been borne out, as we have seen, by the American anthropologists in their attempt to break down the oversimplified interpretations of the older students of myth. In the second place, Freud insists that dreams do not contain intellectual propositions or explanations. When there seems to be an intellectual framework or conceptualization in a dream, we are not to regard it as such but as a functional means of expression, a technique of "displacement," a device for conveying images and emotional impressions. The dream may take into itself a concept, an act of judgment, an intellectual observation, but it becomes a part of the whole dream work. We do not *think* thoughts in a dream: we *see* or *feel* them.[43] For the critic, whether he is considering dreams or myths, it is possible to patch together a series of felt thoughts and to hypostatize them into purely intellectual activity. But to take the hypostatization for the myth or the dream, as did Tylor and Lang, is a mistake. As Freud remarks, "it is the much abused privilege of conscious activity to hide from us all other activities wherever it participates." [44]

It seems to me that Freud must be accorded a very high place by students of myth. His own "scientific myth" of the family is one of the most dramatic and compelling of our time. Psychoanalysis is surely a poetical science. And the reader of this book will perhaps be readily convinced by these words of Lionel Trilling's: "In the eighteenth century Vico had spoken of the metaphorical imagistic language of the earliest stages of culture; it was left for Freud to discover how, in a scientific age, the life of the emotions is lived by figurative formations, and to create, what psychoanalysis is, a science of tropes, of metaphor. . . ." Indeed, as Trilling says, the Freudian psychology shows that the human mind is "in the greater part of its tendency, exactly a poetry making organ." [45] It is a mythmaking organ, too.

Chapter VIII

THE LARGER VIEW

SANTAYANA, whose interpretation of myth is a kind of Epicurean version of nineteenth-century nature worship, tells us that "myth is . . . a natural prologue to philosophy, since the love of ideas is the root of both." [1] This is surely mistaken. Yet we must agree with Santayana that "a good mythology cannot be produced without much culture and intelligence." "Stupidity," as he says, "is not poetical." For us an enduringly interesting or inspiring myth must be at least potentially moral, symbolic, or philosophical. To us, as to the more intelligent savage, the tales of the folk, despite their occasional brilliance and charm, often seem intolerably pedestrian or childish. We must be free, as was the savage priest-thinker, the Greek Stoic, or the Christian father, to interpret the traditional mythology as our moral or intellectual emotions demand. We must be free to so interpret a myth that it comes alive for us in the context of our culture—as special interpretations have in our day made the myths of Oedipus, Joseph, and Philoctetes come alive. Does this mean that our Freudian interpretation of Oedipus is no more nor less justified than the nineteenth-century idea that Oedipus was the sun? In a sense it does, for we have the right to make of myth whatever fulfills a deeply felt human need, so that those who (like the author of "Mythology" in the eighteenth-century *Encyclopédie*) complain that a myth is whatever one's interests lead one to think it is are at least hinting at a pragmatic truth, besides making a satirical remark. Herein lies a justification of those nineteenth-century thinkers who, in common with savage mythmakers of the same temperament, transmuted the human stuff of myth into nature poetry. But there remain certain constant human needs, apart from the parochial configurations of the *Zeitgeist* and apart from differing temperaments, against which we must measure our interpretation of every myth. The danger is to seize upon one facet of the myth, one ghost precipitated from the artistic whole, and suppose that this *is* the myth or the explanation of the myth. A philosophical concept, a moral allegory, a symbol seized upon, cut off from the living whole—this is what I should call a *paramyth*.[2] A paramyth differs from a myth because it is no longer closely involved in the aesthetic emotions, it can no longer furnish that peculiar mythical complication of brilliant excitement, of the terrific play of forces natural and human, of the upshot of the play, of reassurance, of reconciliation. A concept, an allegory, or symbol made for the moment distinguishable but not discrete from its literary vehicle, or a concept, allegory, or symbol disinherited from its matrix but suffused once again with the literary-mythical psychological—only these may be justifiably called "mythical ideas."

Wilhelm Wundt wrote that myths were the result of the "assimilative fusion of psychical elements of differing origins." He compared this complex of mythical elements which we find in any well-developed myth to one of those picture puzzles drawn in the shape of a tree. "In the picture of the foliage of the tree there are sketched the outlines of a human face or of the head of a cat. An uninitiated observer sees at first only the foliage. Not until his attention has been directed to it does he discover the head. Once, however, he has seen the latter, he cannot suppress it, try as he may. . . . It is sometimes but a few indistinct outlines that evoke the picture. The truth is that to a very great extent the observer reads the head into the drawing through the activity of his imagination. Now it is but natural that such an assimilation should be immeasurably enhanced under the influence of the emotions which excite the mythological imagination." [3] To see one form in the whole to the exclusion of others is to see a paramyth. The poet knows the importance of keeping the proper relation between particularized concepts and the aesthetic whole of which they are extrusions;

> O chestnut tree, great rooted blossomer.
> Are you the leaf, the blossom or the bole?
> O body swayed to music, O brightening glance,
> How can we know the dancer from the dance?

Yeats's question is not asked in confusion or despair. It is an assertion that for aesthetic purposes, at least, we should make no sharp separation between the dancer and the dance. What excites the poet is the interaction between the two, and the epiphanies, not the hypostatizations of the dancer.

2.

As we have noticed, Vico, Herder, Malinowski, Radin, and others say that myth need be no more symbolic than any other form of art. It seems to me easier to learn about myth if we stay at the level of metaphor, because there experience is operative; *things are being made;* whereas, at the level of symbol *things have already been made* and we can do naught but contemplate the product, presented to us as an *objet d'art* wrought by we know not what artisan to we know not what purpose. It may possibly be that a statistician (if we could agree with him on what is myth and what is not) could find more symbols in myth than in other kinds of art. There would be small use in his discovery. Nevertheless, thinkers of the rationalistic temperament continue to tell us that myth must be considered as a symbolic mode of thought. The philological nature worshipers and the psychoanalysts have recently been succeeded by a new and increasingly influential group, the semanticists. And I should like to turn briefly to a sensitively written book which is a general assessment of the new semantic, or symbolic, philosophy: Susanne K. Langer's *Philosophy in a New Key.*[4]

Mrs. Langer solicits the attention of students of myth. For, in company with her fellow semanticists, she attributes to myth an importance unprecedented in older philosophies. To her it is a fully accredited mode of ordering human experience, a judgment with which we must heartily agree. Yet we soon learn that semantics, like all scholastic philosophies, rates myth high only as incipient philosophy.

The new philosophy is too eager to embrace the old evolution. Mrs. Langer, writing in a style that would not distress Zeno, says that "primitive thought is not far removed from the dream level." The "best thought" in "primitive societies," she writes, "still bears a childlike stamp. Among certain peoples whom we call 'savage,' the very use of language exhibits a rampant confusion of metaphorical meanings clinging to every symbol, sometimes to the complete obscurance of any reasonable literal meaning." [5] If we accepted, even for a moment, this misleading account of "primitive" thought, we should soon be confused by Mrs. Langer's idea that savages somehow worship "the might of human ideation" and that "fear . . . the driving force in human minds" induces "a demand for a world-picture." What a self-possessed savage he must be who pauses in his terror to philosophize about the nature of the universe! In short, we meet here just the same paradox we noticed in discussing Tylor: the belief that the savage is a kind of insane, or at least childish, rationalist.

Exactly the same paradox limits the usefulness of Mrs. Langer's chapter on "Myth." Myth is, on the one hand, a kind of conscious dream or fantasy belonging to "a passing phase in man's mental history." But on the other hand, the "purpose" of myth is "philosophical"; it is an "embodiment of general ideas"; it is "the primitive phase of metaphysical thought." Surely we can attain only a limited knowledge about a table by observing that it is something like a chair and, then again, something like a house. Myth *may* be like a dream and it *may* be like philosophy, but it *is* art.

That myth is art cannot be very clearly apprehended if we look only at the symbols it precipitates. For the apprehension of art, and the separation of art from dream and philosophy, must of necessity take place at the level of metaphor: i.e., at a level more sentient and operative than the level of symbol.

Since we are interested in distinguishing myth from other orders of experience, we must ask the semanticists if they can help us. How can we tell a mythical symbol from a nonmythical symbol? This question the semanticists cannot answer, beyond talking vaguely about symbols of life, death, birth, sun, moon, rain, fertility, etc. But cannot a mathematician, a historian, a meteorologist, a biologist, or a poet symbolize these things without thereby becoming a mythmaker? If our semanticists tell us that a mythical symbol is one that belongs to "the mythopoeic age," as Mrs. Langer appears to think, we should ask, for one thing, "What about the mythical symbols in our modern poetry?" And we should ask for a closer description of this "mythopoeic age."

It seems to me that the prestige of pragmatic naturalism is not seriously injured by the semanticists. The semanticists have the advantage of a radically limited field of inquiry; it is easy to sound less muddleheaded than a naturalist once you have hypostatized experience into a system of symbols. But the position of Vico and Locke against scholasticism is still the heroic one and has to be taken up again and again.

The semanticists do, however, make one point which naturalists, at least the cruder, utilitarian kind, must take note of. I mean what seems to be the automatic and impractical origin of art, ritual, and language. We learned from Freud that the "pleasure-principle" is influential in the development of man's aesthetic forms. The semanticists advance a similar argument. It is certainly not true that, as Mrs. Langer says, "all magical and ritual practices are hopelessly inappropriate to the preservation and increase of life." Yet it is true that these practices, like art itself, *may* be not only inappropriate but detrimental to life. There is in man a seemingly automatic creativity, a perpetual making of metaphor and symbol which only the subtlest kind of psychology can hope to understand. We are here close to one of those crucial opportunities which excite our times: the opportunity to recapture, in the name of the natural, something apparently beyond the pale.

3.

A number of our most literate critics commonly think of myth as dogma. Two not always separable schools of thought have contributed to this opinion: the Southern School and the followers of T. S. Eliot. A myth or *a* mythology, so we are told, is what modern culture needs because, having lost the guidance of the Christian dogma, we wander at large in the chaos of science and secularism. A new myth, or a new version of the old, must therefore be created to support and guide our belief and our work. To writers of this persuasion myth is something different from and anterior to poetry. It is a general system or framework on which poetry must be based. As one critic puts it, "myth is the indispensable substructure of poetry." But surely the very opposite of this statement is the true formulation: poetry is the indispensable substructure of myth.

Intellectual considerations aside, it is bad strategy to try to make dogma out of myth, for the same reason that it is bad strategy to make philosophy out of myth. Myth is incapable of bearing these burdens, and by insisting that it should, we seem to be discrediting myth. Myth is only art. And we do not think of studying art primarily as dogma or philosophy.

I do not, of course, mean that poets of certain temperament may not beneficially accept a dogma; but that is a personal problem and must not be made a crux of general criticism, much less of programatic crusading.

4.

Those interested in the future of serious literature, including some of its first-rate practitioners (such as D. H. Lawrence, Eliot, Yeats, and Joyce), have in our time insisted that literature must be closely allied with myth. Somehow, it is felt, the creative artist must recapture a certain magical quality, a richness of imagery, a deeper sense of primeval forces, a larger order of aesthetic experience. The difficulty appears to be that our scientific society, secularized and shorn of mystery, is so radically different from the primitive past. It seems impossible to feel any longer, in Yeats's rather sentimental words, as did "the more sensitive people of ancient times." [6] It is a lament which in one form or another has been frequently uttered in the last 150 years.

Yet it is just those writers who most ardently desire the return of the mythmaking of the primitive ages who have, among others, done much to make it difficult. They have projected their most compelling desires, tied them up neatly, labeled them "the mythopoeic age," and consigned them to the oblivion of the remote past. The dogmatic evolutionists have also sealed off the past and represented history as a continuous development away from "the mythopoeic age."

We owe the modern anthropologists a great debt. For they have shown us the falseness of monistic conceptions of primitive society and of cultural history. They have complicated our understanding of primitive psychology so that we can no longer possibly believe that once all thought was mythopoeic or that once all forms of literature were equally and completely mythological. It is perhaps trite to observe that anthropology has shown civilized society to be more like primitive society than we had supposed. But it is not so trite to observe that primitive society now seems more like civilized society than we had supposed. The anthropologists, examining primitive society at firsthand, have accomplished a partial leveling of past and present, just as American pragmatism has in philosophy. We shall cease to lament over the "mythopoeic age" now dead and gone as soon as we realize that as far as can be demonstrated and for all practical purposes there never was such an age. The fact that both savage storytellers and modern writers have wanted to believe in an age when the world was different is highly significant, but not in this connection.

The anthropologists do not, of course, tell us that there are no differences between primitive and civilized thought. There are great differences—consequent upon variations in environment, education, and the apparently whimsical choice of custom and sensibility which differing cultures make. Our infinite specialization and bureaucratization, of course, set us apart from primitive culture. And we have invented numberless surrogates to take the place of primitive ritual, just as we have invented intricate impersonal and automatic systems of security against the injuries of nature and the human enemy. But the difference between primitive and civilized mentality is not absolute; there is no chasm between them, as some scholars have thought. We live in the same world as the savages. Our deepest experience, needs, and aspirations are the same, as surely as the crucial biological and psychic transitions occur in the life of every human being and force culture to take account of them in aesthetic forms.

A savage culture persists in our own. It is here as much as anywhere else. But it is not immediately recognizable unless we modulate our attention, reach out one step beyond the complicated and pigeon-holed fragments—our "heap of broken images," as Eliot says. We do not need to go about the world with Isis, gathering up the fragments of Osiris. For the truth is, he was never more than apparently dismembered. We may be sure that the needs which call forth magic, ritual, and myth are as much with us now when we turn from science to poetry or to the crucial problems of life as they are with the Maori and the Bushman. It is up to the artist to point this out. T. S. Eliot is perfectly right when he remarks that the artist is and should be "more *primitive,* as well as more civilized, than his contemporaries."

The fact that we have no pantheon need worry us no more than the fact that at our particular juncture in history we have lost the traditional Christian dogma. And if we have no Olympus, we may find solace by reflecting that neither had the Greeks—at least not in the form in which we know it, transfixed and embalmed in a handful of texts written at a moment or two in the flux of centuries.

Some scholars and critics have customarily assumed that a poem becomes mythological by referring to a mythology of the past. English poetry has of course repeatedly invoked the Greek gods, but to suppose that a poem becomes mythological by mentioning Zeus or Daphne is certainly misleading. As we have suggested above, literature which "resurrects the past" is mythological only if it does so in a certain way and toward certain ends. Professor Douglas Bush writes at the end of his apparently exhaustive *Mythology and the Romantic Tradition in English Poetry:* "It has been evident throughout this survey . . . that, other things being equal, the mythological poems which are alive are those in which a myth is invested with a modern significance, whether personal or social, and the dead ones are plaster reproductions of the antique." Now, if we are to achieve any clarity in our thinking about myth, we must realize that a "dead" mythological poem is a contradiction in terms. We should rather say that a poem which out of present emotional necessity, "whether personal or social," becomes mythical and then fuses itself with an old myth is a truly mythological poem—but that it does not need the old myth to become mythical.[7]

Those of us who depend on books for our knowledge of the mythologies of the world (Vico resolved to proceed "as if no books existed") have commonly got the impression that mythologies are much more systematic and conservative than they are. An examination of myth as it still lives and functions among a modern primitive people is likely to show a surprising lack of homogeneity. The same myth takes on the differing forms given it by different raconteurs; when a single myth appears among different peoples or endures over a period of time among one people, it will assume a variety of forms and nuances according to a variety of aesthetic climates—and this despite the savage's rather compulsive fear of or lack of interest in change. As Radin says, "over and above the precise form in which he [the storyteller] obtains the myth stands his relation as an artist to the dramatic situations contained in it and to his audience." [8] The emotional necessity of myth is constant; the forms of myth are not. A myth concerning the supernatural birth of a dead woman's son was recorded by Professor Boas on Vancouver Island in 1888 and again in 1900; but in 1931 no one on the island remembered the story.[9] We may suppose that Herder was right to insist that the ancient myth was dynamic and changeable and that any single "received" representation of it was likely to be misleading.

The concept of "survivals" advanced by Tylor, Lang, Frazer, and others is not considered very useful by the American anthropologists. A "survival," to the older writers, meant an irrational custom or rite which persisted through the changes of history and "survived" in modern culture, often seeming to be at great variance with the prevailing modes of behavior. The collections of European folk tales made in the nineteenth century were a strong stimulus to this theory. The emphasis on "survivals" was thus partly accidental. European folk tales are more conservative and homogeneous than most. They were recorded in a time of revolutionary change; and, opposed to the new industrial culture in which they were collected and written down, they seemed to bespeak a tremendous time lag.[10] But even if this apparent time lag forced such a schism between primitive and modern European culture as it seemed to, we should still have to consider it a parochial phenomenon in the history of the world. The irrational elements of myth are not so much survivals of primeval conditions as the constantly repeated and regenerated motifs of the mythmaker's imagination, whether he is primeval or modern.

An extensive and detailed analysis of poetry as myth, and the comprehension of our poetic tradition which such an analysis might bring, is beyond the scope of the present volume. But I think the general arguments of the book require a measure of concrete illustration. I have selected the poems discussed below according to no principle but a desire to say something coherent about the three schools of poetry which have meant most to me: the Metaphysical, the Romantic, and (for lack of a better term) the Modern.[11] For if our mythical method suggests a view of our poetical heritage and future, it is a larger view than is offered by the inspiration and discipline of any particular school of poets. The categories I use in what follows are the ones developed in Chapter VI.

5.

I think we honor Donne partly for the dark mysteriousness with which he invests human life and for the kind of hieratic ritual his poems sometimes seem to perform. For example the rich and stately "Epithalamion made at Lincolnes Inne." The purpose of this poem, I should say, is to defend the institution of marriage against the wastage of apathy and artificiality. But Donne does not *argue* in defense of marriage on ethical, religious, or social grounds. He reasserts the vital *reality* of marriage as a custom and a ritual. To use Malinowski's words, he "resurrects primeval reality." His poem is mythical because a "rite, ceremony, or a social or moral rule demands justification, warrant of antiquity, reality, and sanctity."

This morning, as Donne says, a "faire Bride" leaves a bed which is "solitary" for the last time. "To night" she will "put on perfection, and a womans name" (the repetition of this line as a refrain emphasizes the ritualism of the poem). At the beginning Donne says that "the Sun-Beames in the East are spred"; and though he does not yet employ this image mythically, we feel an incipient largeness of scene. The sunbeams are not just decorations; they are there to tell us that the forces of the universe attend upon the ritual, a fact which Donne makes explicit in the last stanza. In the second stanza the poet invokes the

> Daughters of London, you which bee
> Our Golden Mines, and furnish'd Treasurie,
> You which are Angels, yet still bring with you
> Thousands of Angels on your marriage daies. . . .

The Daughters of London, of course, are actual young women. But, at the same time, they are Angels, and they are summoned for a very specific purpose:

> Help with your presence and device to praise
> These rites.

They are the "real," the dynamic, the aesthetic, the magical fact, invoked to make a particular marriage a real fact of the same order. (The word "presence," of course, means something which is momentously and uncannily present, not just objectively and statically so.) Donne further exhorts the Daughters of London:

> Conceitedly dress her, and be assign'd
> By you, fit place for every flower and jewell,
> Make her for love fit fewell
>   As gay as Flora, and as rich as Inde;
> So may shee faire, rich, glad, and in nothing lame,
> *To day put on perfection, and a womans name.*

The angelic Daughters do not dress the Bride in clothes and flowers and jewels only, but in their own virtue. By a kind of contagious magic, the Bride puts on mythical quality. She is "in nothing lame"; she is perfection—a Being full of mysterious potencies and felicities—an adept Functionary of earth's most wonderful realities.

That Donne means to make the Bride a mythical Being becomes unquestionably clear in the last stanza:

> Even like a faithfull man content,
> That this life for a better should be spent,
>   So, shee a mothers rich style doth preferre,
> And at the Bridegroomes wish'd approach doth lye,
> Like an appointed lambe, when tenderly
>   The priest comes on his knees t'embowell her;
>   Now sleep or watch with more joy; and O light
> Of heaven, to morrow rise thou hot, and early;
> This Sun will love so dearely
>   Her rest, that long, long we shall want her sight. . . .

The sacrificial lamb is an object of awe and wonder. The redness of its bloody bowels and their dark potency—fiat of divination or a promise of fertility—fuse into a total impression of reality, which is reinforced and generalized by "the light—Of heaven" which rises "hot" and "loves." The magical purpose of the metaphor is completed in the imaginative fusion of the lamb with the Bride and the elevation of the Bride to mythical status. Donne attests to the fact that the metaphor is indeed *magical*:

> Wonders are wrought, for shee which had no maime,
> *To night puts on perfection, and a womans name.*

It is an intellectual paradox and witticism that she who was already perfect has tonight put on perfection. But if, as I think we must, we take Donne to mean something like "she who was not wounded has now been wounded and yet is unwounded," then we see that the Bride is none other than the magical creature of the myths who receives a miraculous wound that is no injury but a new perfection. More, she exemplifies what Toynbee calls "withdrawal-and-return." She withdraws in the dark night of her passions to a "rest" so complete "that long, long we shall want her sight"; and she returns to the world, transfigured. The myth of the hero-god's death and resurrection achieves many strange and wonderful forms in Donne's poems.

Surely, this is a mythical poem, and much of its excitement is a consequence of Donne's conscious exploitation of the mythical method. He realizes the marvelous juxtapositions and contrasts he can make by combining careful references to concrete objects ("warme balme-breathing thigh," "sheets," "cradle") with the forces, at once brutal and superhuman, whose aid he solicits. Only in such a poem could the word "tenderly" (in "tenderly/ The priest comes on his knees") take on such ironic power.

And surely this is a hard-working poem, a poem that labors and gropes after the mythical. There is no prefabricated myth upon whose bosom the poem languishes. Donne's myth is Donne's poem when it achieves a certain kind of excellence.

Wordsworth's "Ode: Intimations of Immortality" has been subjected to a very subtle and illuminating analysis by Lionel Trilling.[12] Trilling's point is that in the "Ode" Wordsworth "is talking about something common to us all, the development of the sense of reality." I should like to turn briefly to Wordsworth's "Resolution and Independence" and show that this poem, too, is about the sense of reality. The usual notion about this poem seems to be that Wordsworth, as poets will, has become despondent. He is lonesome and so poor that he must postpone his marriage, and he fears that the poet's lot is to know a measure of "gladness" in his youth and to sink but too soon into "madness." A walk over the moors, however, and an encounter with a noble and resolute old Leech-gatherer restore his self-confidence and his inspiration. But let us look more closely at the poem. Trilling speaks of the passage on pre-existence in the "Ode" as "a very serious conceit . . . intended to give a high value to . . . natural experience." There is such a conceit, or myth, in "Resolution and Independence," and it serves just the same purpose.

Wordsworth's poem is not an exercise in romantic melancholy. As the poet walks out on a beautiful, bright morning, he is, to be sure, oppressed with his worldly condition: his "solitude," his "distress," his "poverty." But I do not think these words indicate the full content of his despondency:

> . . . as it sometimes chanceth, from the might
> Of joy in minds that can no further go,
> As high as we have mounted in delight
> In our dejection do we sink as low;
> To me that morning did it happen so;
> And fears and fancies thick upon me came;
> Dim sadness—and blind thoughts, I knew not, nor could name.

Notice that Wordsworth is talking of "minds"; his sadness is "dim"; his thoughts are "blind." In a later stanza we hear that he is "perplexed," and in writing about his poem Wordsworth says specifically that what he gains from meeting the Leech-gatherer is "new insight." The sense of the reality of natural experience, which Wordsworth cherishes above all else, suddenly leaves him. When he speaks of "madness" in an ensuing stanza, he is not using a trope. There is nothing sentimental or soft in the word. He means insanity: the abyss opens before him. The two following stanzas demonstrate the dilemma Wordsworth is in:

> I heard the sky-lark warbling in the sky;
> And I bethought me of the playful hare:
> Even such a happy Child of earth am I;
> Even as these blissful creatures do I fare;
> Far from the world I walk, and from all care;
> But there may come another day to me—
> Solitude, pain of heart, distress, and poverty.

> My whole life I have lived in pleasant thought,
> As if life's business were a summer mood;

> As if all needful things would come unsought
> To genial faith, still rich in genial good;
> But how can he expect that others should
> Build for him, sow for him, and at his call
> Love him, who for himself will take no heed at all?

Now, these lines are, to be sure, full of apprehension concerning the poet's worldly estate and full of self-blame. But what is responsible for "the fear that kills," the sudden wave of "fears and fancies," that has come over the poet? Is it not that he perceives a scale of values other than his own and that he suddenly fears that the other scale is the true reality and that if this is so, he is lost in an appalling emptiness. Wordsworth's sense of reality, the whole foundation of his sanity and productiveness, is called into question. For the moment a rival reality presents itself. The word "resolution" in the title of the poem does not mean anything ethical like "the determination to carry on." It means, I think, the resolution of a dilemma, the banishment of a false reality, the reassertion of a true reality. And the true reality is reasserted mythically.

The old Leech-gatherer appears to Wordsworth as a revelation. It is so felicitous a revelation that it seems to have happened out of the necessity of Wordsworth's dilemma. The appearance of the old man may be "a leading from above, a something given." The reason why the Leech-gatherer affects Wordsworth so strongly is that, as we should say, he has *mana*. He is a roughhewn man of flesh and blood, but he is also a vehicle of natural forces and a visitor from the primeval world ("like a man from some far region sent"). As Malinowski might put it, he is "a primeval, greater and more relevant reality by which the present life, fates and activities of mankind are determined."

> As a huge stone is sometimes seen to lie
> Couched on the bald top of an eminence;
> Wonder to all who do the same espy,
> By what means it could thither come, and whence;
> So that it seems a thing endued with sense:
> Like a sea-beast crawled forth, that on a shelf
> Of rock or sand reposeth, there to sun itself;

Such seemed this Man, not all alive nor dead,
Nor all asleep—in his extreme old age:
His body was bent double, feet and head
Coming together in life's pilgrimage;
As if some dire constraint of pain, or rage
Of sickness felt by him in times long past,
A more than human weight upon his frame had cast.

I think it important that Wordsworth attributes to the Leech-gatherer just that sense of the reality of nature which the poet himself fears that he may have lost. The Leech-gatherer, with his "yet-vivid eyes," is able to "con" the ponds and pools of water "as if he had been reading in a book." And Wordsworth describes the old man's mind as "firm."

Yet the poet does not recover his own sense of natural reality by observing the old man and emulating him. The vision in which the old man appears (for it *is* a vision) is to Wordsworth the essence of reality. The universe acquires vibrancy and vitality; things are set in motion again by the presence of the Leech-gatherer. "Natural experience," which had for a moment become flat and cold, again acquires a "high value."

The myth in "Resolution and Independence" performs a less obviously cultural function than the myth in Donne's "Epithalamion." Yet the mythical element of the poem does not perform a purely psychological purpose. I agree with Mr. Trilling that in the "Ode" Wordsworth is not speaking so much of the particular experience of poets as of human experience generally. "Resolution and Independence," however, is a cultural poem: it deals with "Poets" (Wordsworth uses the capital letter) and the poet's place in a hostile economic situation. It is characteristic of Wordsworth that he should stress the poet's psychology rather than speak of the poet as a necessary or time-honored cultural phenomenon. Nevertheless, Wordsworth's poem is a justification of the poet and a reassertion of the poet's view of things.

6.

We have said that myth preserves the magical view of things—
that it keeps the magician's world "from falling apart," and that it
reaffirms the brilliancy and drama of life. It performs the same
function for the poet. I shall try to make clear what I mean by
examining two poems, one by Yeats and one by Donne.

Yeats's famous poem "Among School Children" is a good example
of the successful use of myth. The poem begins thus:

> I walk through the long schoolroom questioning;
> A kind old nun in a white hood replies;
> The children learn to cipher and to sing,
> To study reading-books and history,
> To cut and sew, be neat in everything
> In the best modern way—the children's eyes
> In momentary wonder stare upon
> A sixty-year-old smiling public man.

This is discursive writing, an arrangement of details and properties,
the statement of a problem (for the poet walks "questioning"). The
problem of the poet is how to discover in the given situation the
energy and order of a coherent poetic statement. The poet needs
an incandescent focus around which to consolidate and realize his
discursive thoughts and more or less random emotions. In short,
he needs a myth. The myth must rise out of the necessity of the
poem, for it cannot be *any* myth that occurs to the poet. The myth
is one of Yeats's favorites. And though it takes its name and some
of its strength from the myth of Leda and the Swan, it is largely of
Yeats's own creation.

> I dream of a Ledaean body, bent
> Above a sinking fire, a tale that she
> Told of a harsh reproof, or trivial event
> That changed some childish day to tragedy—
> Told, and it seemed that our two natures blent
> Into a sphere from youthful sympathy,
> Or else, to alter Plato's parable,
> Into the yolk and white of the one shell.

Now, the "Ledaean body" is no doubt Yeats's beloved revolutionary, Maud Gonne; but she is Maud Gonne mythicized. She is possessed of powers given her by the father of the gods. She has been "mastered by the brute blood of the air," as Yeats says in his sonnet called "Leda and the Swan," and she has put on his "power" and perhaps his "knowledge." In a kind of epiphany she does for the incipiently poetic situation sketched in the first stanza of "Among School Children" what the mind of Yeats cannot do as long as it limits itself to discursive thought. She shows that "some childish day" may be "tragedy." Realizing this and believing it, Yeats is able to give a "high value" to the reflections about life which appear in the succeeding stanzas. "Two natures blent," as he says. And this is the basic metaphor of myth.

What I venture to call the "epiphany" does not fulfill its mission at one stroke. Perhaps the vision is for the moment too etherial; it must be further naturalized; the mystery, the awfulness, the brilliancy must be seen *in* the children:

> And thinking of that fit of grief or rage
> I look upon one child or t'other there
> And wonder if she stood so at that age—
> For even daughters of the swan can share
> Something of every paddler's heritage—
> And had that color upon cheek or hair. . . .

This momentary pause, while things are being realized, is all that is required to ensure the success of the mythical fusion:

> And thereupon my heart is driven wild:
> She stands before me as a living child.

The rest of the poem, which we cannot consider here, gathers speed toward its transcendant conclusion on the strength of this burst of power. It is a resolution of the possibilities of the subject matter into certain beautiful images which embody certain moral and metaphysical speculations.

Can we learn anything about the conceits of Donne by the mythical method? I think most readers of Donne feel that there is something vaguely mythical about some of his striking metaphors, his sudden concentration of passion and thought in a conceit. Such a conceit as "oft did we grow/To be two Chaosses" surely partakes somehow of myth.

This conceit occurs in "A nocturnall upon S. Lucies day," a poem lamenting the death of the poet's lady and describing his desolation of spirit. We are told that the lovers grew to be "two Chaosses" whenever they "did show/Care to ought else" but each other. Donne means to say that the lovers became *like* chaos; they were distraught, life became meaningless. But I think he also means to say that they actually degenerated into chaos, uncreated, universal chaos; and, furthermore, that the universe itself became chaos, when the two lovers turned from each other.

It is a favorite thought of Donne's that the order of the universe depends on certain individual human beings. For example, in "The Canonization" we hear of the lovers "who did the whole worlds soule contract"; in "An Anatomy of the World," Donne speaks of the young girl

> . . . to whom this world must itself refer
> As suburbs or the microcosm of her.

And we learn that when the girl died, "all coherence" in the world is "gone" because of the death of her

> . . . that had all magnetic force alone
> To draw and fasten sundered parts in one.

Now, by saying that the lovers grew "to be two Chaosses" Donne gives them a mythical value. His problem is how to "resurrect the reality" of the lovers' turning from each other, how to get at the true poignancy of feeling. He has succeeded by borrowing, so to speak, the terrible destructive forces of the uncreated universe and fusing them with a concrete human activity. The conceit, or myth, lends the poem a significance and brilliancy which more discursive language could not hope to equal. Those who suppose that the myths in Donne's poems are confined to the Christian myth and an occasional reference to the classics overlook a great deal. Very often, I think, the mystery and poignancy of Donne's poems can be understood by considering his conceits as a kind of shorthand myth.

It should not surprise us, by the way, that in his poetry Donne is much more the magician than the priest. For him, the dynamism of the world, as well as its order, depends on human beings. When his beloved dies, as Donne tells us in the "Nocturnall upon S. Lucies day," "the worlds whole sap is sunke." And when the young girl in the "Anatomy of the World" dies, "the element of fire is quite put out" and "the world's spent." The forces of the universe may be compelled to do man's bidding by a verbal technique (the poet's "magic"), because they depend for their very life on human emotions and desires.

7.

In Chapter VI we pointed out that the clash between magic and religion in primitive society was psychologically a clash between the ego, which desires to envelop and coerce the objective world, and gods and spirits, those objectively conceived powers which seek to coerce nature and man. And we suggested that myth was that kind of poetry which reconciles these opposing forces "by making them interact coercively toward a common end."

Wordsworth, I think, conceived of poetry as I here conceive of myth. In Book i of *The Prelude* he writes: [13]

> For I, methought, while the sweet breath of heaven
> Was blowing on my body, felt within
> A correspondent breeze, that gently moved
> With quickening virtue, but is now become
> A tempest, a redundant energy,
> Vexing its own creation. Thanks to both,
> And their congenial powers, that, while they join
> In breaking up a long-continued frost,
> Bring with them vernal promises, the
> Hope of active days . . .
> Vespers and matins of harmonious verse.

The harmonious activity of an internal and an external power which breaks the frost allows the poet to write poetry. "Frost" means to Wordsworth apathy or frustration, but also, as in line 132 of the "Ode," it means the "earthly freight" of "custom." Does he not mean that until these "powers" become "congenial," the "frost" of ordinary life is upon him, his creative capacities are paralyzed by disharmonies and tensions, but that when they join, he attains, as he says elsewhere, "harmony, and the deep power of joy," and he is able to see "into the life of things."?

In Wordsworth's poetry we often miss the sense of the horror and awfulness of "nature." Yet this sense is not entirely lacking. Wordsworth tells us that he grew up "fostered alike by beauty and by fear" (all quotations are from Book i of *The Prelude* unless otherwise noted). And he sometimes tries to describe how the "extrinsic passion" of nature could become for him a cosmic antagonist to be feared and fought. The famous account of the illicitly borrowed rowboat and the mountain which rears up to terrify the miscreant is something more, I think, than a Protestant confession of guilt, just as the "huge peak, black and huge" is something more than a stern, mythicized schoolmaster. What appalls the poet is that the mountain suddenly seems to be "with voluntary power instinct," to have a "purpose of its own." Things "fall apart" before the horrified gaze of a human being who has tried to encompass and control the universe with a too easy, an immature magic. "Those first affinities that fit/Our new existence to existing things" prove inadequate to their task. God has confronted the poet and called his subjectivism into question.

Wordsworth shows little interest in the edifying moral of the story: he is interested in larger questions. He is telling us that an overpowering *religious* experience had made him desolate by sweeping the universe frighteningly clean of the friendly "shapes" with which he had peopled it and filling it instead with predatory and uncontrollable "forms":

> . . . after I had seen
> That spectacle, for many days, my brain
> Worked with a dim and undetermined sense
> Of unknown modes of being; o'er my thoughts
> There hung a darkness, call it solitude
> Or blank desertion. No familiar shapes
> Remained, no pleasant images of trees,
> Of sea or sky, no colours of green fields;
> But huge and mighty forms, that do not live

Like living men, moved slowly through the mind
By day, and were a trouble to my dreams.

According to Wordsworth, it is the office of the poetic "Imagination"
to resolve the dilemma, to reconcile the known with "the unknown
modes of being." He believes that poetry can do this, for, as he says,

> . . . there is a dark
> Inscrutable workmanship that reconciles
> Discordant elements, makes them cling together
> In one society.

This "dark inscrutable workmanship" is what I call the Promethean
function of myth.

Sometimes Wordsworth's Promethean workmanship was able to
reconcile familiar shapes with huge and mighty forms in myths
whose brilliancy modern criticism does not seem generally to detect. For example, the myth of the phantasmal Arab in Book v of
The Prelude. This myth is based on a dream Wordsworth had had
after falling asleep in a cave by the sea, where he had gone to read
Cervantes. Wordsworth tells us that a figure riding on a camel
appeared to him out of a "sandy wilderness, all black and void."
The "new-comer" seemed to be an Arab, but he was also Don
Quixote. He carried a lance, a stone, and a resplendent shell. As he
beholds the Arab with his strange lumber, Wordsworth loses "the
distress and fear" with which the desert had first filled him, and
contemplating the "surpassing brightness" of the vision, he "re-
joices" and thinks that the Arab is a guide who will lead him through
the desert "with unerring skill." The Arab tells the poet that the
stone is a book, Euclid's "Elements," which holds

> . . . acquaintance with the stars,
> And [weds] soul to soul in purest bond
> Of reason, undisturbed by space or time.

The shell is also a book; it is an "Ode" which utters "a loud prophetic blast of harmony." It is a "god, yea many gods." It has voices
"more than all the winds" and "power/To exhilarate the spirit," and
to soothe the heart. It speaks in an unknown tongue, but its prophecy

is strangely intelligible. In the midst of the desert it prophesies death
by water. The "children" who "sport upon the shore,/And hear the
mighty waters rolling evermore" in that profound passage of the
"Intimations Ode" are to be overwhelmed "with the fleet waters
of a drowning world:"

> Destruction to the children of the earth
> By deluge, now at hand.

The Arab hurries on. He must bury the stone and the shell in the
earth.

The poet feels a strong desire to "cleave unto this man" and to
"share his enterprize." He follows the Arab, who has begun to ride
across "the waste," looking frequently over his shoulder and "grasp-
ing his twofold treasure.—Lance at rest. . . ." The Arab's face (he
is now more clearly identified with Don Quixote) grows more and
more disturbed as he looks back. The poet, still following, also looks
back; he sees "a bed of glittering light" diffused "over half the
wilderness." "It is the waters of the deep/Gathering upon us," says
the Arab-Quixote, and the camel quickens his "unwieldy" gait
across the desert, leaving Wordsworth in the path of "the fleet
waters."

The immediate effect of this dreamlike myth is terror, but its long-
range, total effect is calmness and resolution. "Reason did lie couched
in the blind and awful lair/Of such a madness." And Wordsworth
adds that in sober contemplation "I could share

> That maniac's fond anxiety, and go
> Upon like errand.

Indeed, he does go upon like errand, for he finds that the "strong
enchantment" of his mythical vision comes upon him whenever he
takes up a volume of Shakespeare or Milton. Whole chaosses of
experience are made magically real, are fused "in one society" by the
"dark inscrutable workmanship" of Wordsworth's productive
years.

We might note, furthermore, that, just as in "Resolution and
Independence," the myth of the Arab asserts Wordsworth's poetic
vision of reality as against other visions:

Enow there are on earth to take in charge
Their wives, their children, and their virgin loves,
Or whatsoever else the heart hold dear;
Enow to stir for these. . . .

Wordsworth will take the sterner vision of the world which he sees in the "maniac's fond anxiety." For him, that is reality.

Does not the fate of Wordsworth confirm our views? When he is no longer able to make capital out of the conflicting claims of magic and religion and allows himself to be absorbed from the one into the other, he loses the mythmaking power. In order to write "The Ecclesiastical Sonnets" he has to lose the sense of what Arnold accurately called "natural magic." He is left with religion and his barren poems. Wordsworth is a hero during the brief moment of his most brilliant deeds on the contested field, but as he had emerged from the anonymity of the multitudinous Magicians, so he quickly recedes into the anonymous company of the Religious.

W. H. Auden's "In Sickness and in Health" is a poem about the difficulty of married love in the modern world. It raises some of the questions about morality, psychology, and religion faced by two (apparently) recently married friends of the poet. I should like to consider the poem as Auden's attempt to find the counterpoise between animal nature and the Divine which the lovers must attain if they are to make their marriage decent and workable. It is a poem of tensions, and these tensions are resolved because the lovers attain that level of experience where they become, in the necessary degree, mythical.

At the opening of the poem there is a warning against the "Black/Dog" that "leaps upon the individual back." He is the "desolation" and the "famine" of

Those inarticulate wastes where dwell
Our howling appetites.

He is a warning against the "land of condors, sick cattle, and dead flies" from which

. . . figures of destruction unawares
Jump out on Love's imagination
And chase away the castles and the bears.

The "figures of destruction," we may assume, are the uncreated myths of our time—the repressed ghosts that wound from within because we have not projected our emotions into adequate myths, the latter being here symbolized by "the castles and the bears." Auden tells us in the first four stanzas of his poem that married love in our time is a momentous undertaking and that it requires "huge resources" to make out of love—which may so easily become an "inarticulate waste"—something creative and useful.

The next three stanzas explore the fate of love unguided by any principle other than that of nature, and the lovers are warned that "Nature by nature in unnature ends." There are two ways in which human love may meet this fate: the way of Tristan and Isolde, who use love in order to escape life, who

> . . . perish lest Brangaene's worldly cry
> Should sober their cerebral ecstasy;

and the way of Don Juan, who is "so terrified of death" that he uses love as a means of escaping it, and so, "trapped in . . . vile affections,"

> . . . a helpless, blind,
> Unhappy spook, he haunts the urinals,
> Existing solely by their miracles.

Out of the "syllogistic nightmare" of these two perversions comes the impulse to devote the sexual energies to war and power politics. And this brings love to the final state of "unnature":

> New Machiavellis flying through the air
> Express a metaphysical despair,
> Murder their last voluptuous sensation,
> All passion in one passionate negation.

This is the larger setting of the problem. The next stanza is more poignant, closer home to the married love of the intellectual,

> Beloved, we are always in the wrong,
> Handling so clumsily our stupid lives,
> Suffering too little or too long,
> Too careful even in our selfish loves:

The decorative manias we obey
Die in grimaces round us every day,
Yet through their tohu-bohu comes a voice
Which utters an absurd command—Rejoice.

At this point in the poem the lovers are made to face God and to consider what must be their relation to Him. (Auden uses a very old but a very good argument: God must be believed in *because* of the absurdity of believing in Him.) The injunction to Rejoice is followed by a beautiful, somewhat Yeatsian stanza in praise of God:

> *What talent for the makeshift thought*
> *A living corpus out of odds and ends?*
> *What pedagogic patience taught*
> *Pre-occupied and savage elements*
> *To dance into a segregated charm?*
> *Who showed the whirlwind how to be an arm,*
> *And gardened from the wilderness of space*
> *The sensual properties of one dear face?*

The rest of the poem as it seems to me, takes its energy and significance from the tensions set up by the introduction of the religious theme. The lovers must believe that there is a god and that they "exist by grace," though by grace "of the Absurd." Two forces oppose each other: the ego and God. In short, we find the ancient antagonists—magic and religion—at war in Auden's poem. The ego still asserts its power over nature, still asserts freedom of the will, still seeks, once a god is established, to coerce him. God claims His right to coerce the human ego, to assert the rule of external Necessity. The poet, turned mythmaker, tries to reconcile the clashing forces and to make useful experience, experience favorable to the preservation of human life, out of the tensions of the dilemma.

God is not called God in this poem. He is adored, but as in the italicized stanza quoted above, He is adored in questions. He is called "Love," "Essence of creation," "Fate," "talent," "patience," "arm," and even *"Felix Osculum."* The poet insists that the lovers believe in a pragmatic god—one who is named diversely with names ranging from the anthropomorphic "arm" to the mystic "Essence of creation" according to the various purposes he fulfills. The god of the poem strains away from earth, but the ego bends him to its will. He is never allowed to become enduringly supernatural.

The lovers are warned not to suppose that they themselves are godlike. They employ the "arbitrary circle of a vow"

> . . . lest we manufacture in our flesh
> The lie of our divinity. . . .

They agree to beware of compulsive injury to the self, not to commit "That sin of the high-minded, sublimation," but to submit instead to the control which religion can put upon the unconscious. They resolve to

> . . . seek Thee always in Thy substances,
> Till the performance of those offices
> Our bodies, Thine opaque enigmas, do
> Configure Thy transparent justice too.

That is to say, they resolve to abandon the destructive kind of compulsion by which the "reason . . . damns the soul" and devote themselves to a magic and ritual of sexual love which, by partaking of the divine order of things, assures a constructive sublimation.

The magic ritual must not be allowed to degenerate into too crude a form: the lovers must take care

> Lest animal bias should decline our wish
> For Thy perfection to identify
> Thee with Thy things, to worship fish. . . .

The ritual must solicit the "light" of divine "Love," must fuse it with the "intellectual motions" of the lovers so as to "excite" "such intense vibration"

> That we give forth a quiet none can tell
> From that in which the lichens live so well.

Now, here surely the lovers find their counterpoise. A preternatural force fuses with a human activity and the actors assume just that calm potency, that grandeur and mysteriousness of great power at rest, which we think is one aspect of the mythical. The poem here places the lovers at the level of myth; they become mythical Beings.

They achieve what the "true lovers" of whom Auden speaks in his "New Year Letter" hope to find: a "language and a myth." What they think and feel resolves into useful experience the tensions set up by the struggle between those forces which we broadly designate as magic and religion. Tristan and Isolde make love into an escape from life, Don Juan makes it an escape from death, the lovers in Auden's poem make it *a means of life,* such life as the complex soul must live. The poem ends with an incantatory restatement of the resolution which has been achieved; it is a prayer to but also a limitation upon the divine Power:

> O hold us to the voluntary way.

Perhaps I have said enough to suggest that if "the mythical method" is useful at all in helping us to assess our poetical heritage and detect the paths criticism can most fruitfully take in the future, it is useful in a large and hopeful sense. We may be sure, at least, that it entails a great deal more than Mr. Eliot's melancholy Fisher King supposed—who tried to shore up his ruins with fragments of the past. I find reason for hope in my belief that poetry is a primitive, a fundamental product of man's mind and that wherever it has appeared it has striven against human bias and exclusiveness to transfigure itself into myth.

NOTES

NOTES FOR FOREWORD

[1] "Folklore," *Encyclopedia of Social Sciences* (New York, 1931), VI, 292.

[2] A more exhaustive account is Otto Gruppe's *Geschichte der Klassischen Mythologie und Religionsgeschichte während des Mittelalters im Abendland und während der Neuzeit* (Leipzig, 1921). This has the bias of the Greek scholar and is mercilessly bibliographical. Two works by modern Catholic scholars are useful: H. Pinard de la Boullaye, "Son Histoire dans le monde occidental," Vol. I of *L'Etude comparée des Religions* (Paris, 1929); and W. Schmidt, *The Growth and Origin of Religion: Facts and Theories*, tr. by H. J. Rose (London, 1931). See also J. M. Robertson, *Christianity and Mythology* (London, 1910).

NOTES FOR CHAPTER I

TRADITIONAL VIEWS OF MYTH

[1] George Grote, *History of Greece* (London, 1903), I, 356.

[2] Cf. de la Boullaye, *L'Etude comparée*, I, 19.

[3] See E. Zeller, *The Stoics, Epicureans, and Sceptics*, tr. by O. J. Reichel (London, 1892), 354–68.

[4] The translation (with minor changes) of C. G. Osgood, *Boccaccio on Poetry* (Princeton, 1930), 12.

[5] James Spedding, R. L. Ellis, D. D. Heath, *The Works of Francis Bacon* (Boston, 1860–64), XIII, 159–62.

[6] On Conti and Bacon, see C. W. Lemmi, *The Classic Deities in Bacon* (Baltimore, 1933).

[7] See the remnant of Euhemerus' lost work preserved in the *Praeparatio Evangelica* of Eusebius, tr. by E. H. Gifford (Oxford, 1903), II, ii. Eusebius' account is based partly on Diodorus Siculus *Fragmenta* vi. 2. A description by Euhemerus of "Panchaea" as a political utopia is to be found in Diodorus, *The Library of History*, tr. by C. H. Oldfather (London, 1939), V, 41–46.

[8] This episode is recounted in Lactantius *Divin. Inst.* i. 11, 13; cited by Paul Decharmé, *La Critique des Traditions Religieuses chez les Grecs* (Paris, 1904), 379. This book should be consulted on the whole question of Greek and Roman criticism of the ancient myth.

[9] Otto Gruppe, *Griechische Mythologie* (Munich, 1906), 1514. A. B. Cook, on the other hand, thinks we incline to underestimate the seriousness of Euhemerus. Though of course rejecting Euhemerus' theory of the origin of Zeus, he points out that it attains a certain substantiality from the ancient Minoan kings, who were regarded as Zeus on earth. *Zeus* (Cambridge, 1914), I, 662.

[10] *Isis and Osiris*, cited in Eusebius (Gifford, tr.), *Praeparatio Evangelica*, IV, 58.

[11] Bk. viii, 26.

[12] Vol. II, 218, *passim*.

[13] Schmidt (Rose, tr.), *Origin and Growth of Religion*, 20 ff.

¹⁴ De la Boullaye, *L'Etude comparée*, I, 170 ff.

¹⁵ *Geographiae Sacrae*, I, 1, 8; cited in Noah Webster, "Origin of Mythology," *Memoirs of the Connecticut Academy* (New Haven, 1810), I, 175–216. Webster was a determined foe of the Hebraists. Given his narrowly etymological method of tracing the classical gods back to Celtic names for moral qualities and natural phenomena, Webster is an eminently sane mythologist.

¹⁶ Schmidt (Rose, tr.), *Origin and Growth of Religion*, 23–24.

¹⁷ Robertson Smith, *Lectures on the Religion of the Semites* (London, 1894), vi; and *Folklore in the Old Testament* (London, 1919), I, viii.

¹⁸ Down to the nineteenth century "fable" was generally used for our word "myth."

¹⁹ *Essay Concerning Human Understanding*, iv, 11, 17.

²⁰ "The Whole History of Navigation," preface to *Churchill's Voyages*.

NOTES FOR CHAPTER II

MYTH IN THE ENLIGHTENMENT

¹ One might advance the claim to this distinction of an earlier skeptic than Fontenelle. See La Mothe le Vayer, *Deux Dialogues faits à l'imitation des anciens* (1630).

² Ed. by J. R. Carré (Paris, 1932). This essay is a by-product of Fontenelle's *Sur l'Histoire*, Carré believes it was conceived before 1680. It was written between 1691 and 1699, and was published in 1724.

³ (London, 1906), II, 339.

⁴ In his fifth Dialogue of the Dead, Fontenelle makes Homer converse with Aesop. Aesop is surprised to find that Homer was not consciously writing fables:

Ae. "What! did you never intend to imply great mysteries in your works?"

H. "Alas, not I."

Aesop finds it difficult to believe that Homer's poems were attempts at setting down objective truth as it was conceived in that era and that Homer should expect his readers to take his fables literally. Aesop is seized with a sudden fear that people will take his own fables at their face value.

⁵ Tr. anon. (London, 1708).

⁶ Cf. *Les moeurs des sauvages Amériquains, comparées aux moeurs des premiers temps* (1724), by Joseph Lafitau, a Jesuit missionary to Canada: "I vow that if the ancient authors have given me reason to support certain conjectures touching the savages, the customs of the savages have helped me more easily to understand and explain many things which are in the ancient authors." This work contains a vast and confused mass of anthropological information about primitive tribes and classical peoples—an eighteenth-century *Golden Bough*. It was well known later in the century; for example, to Voltaire and Herder.

⁷ *Histoire des Oracles, Oeuvres* (Paris, 1825), III, 83. First published in 1687, this book was a translation of the *De Oraculis* of the Dutch Protestant Van Dale, the standard work on oracles during the Enlightenment. The book maintains negatively that oracles cannot be attributed to demons and that the oracles did not disappear with the coming of Christ, and positively that the Catholic Church is responsible for perpetuating primitive myth and magic.

⁸ Tr. by Mrs. Aphra Behn and others (London, 1801).

⁹ *The Dictionary Historical and Critical of Mr. Peter Bayle*, (2d ed.; London, 1738), IV, 861.

[10] See article on David in Bayle, *Dictionary*.

[11] *Miscellaneous Reflections, Occasioned by the Comet which Appeared in December, 1680* (London, 1708), I, 138.

[12] Vol. IV, 584.

[13] His sources of knowledge about Adonis are, among others, Augustine, Lucian, Ammianus Marcellinus, Jerome, Cyril, Plutarch.

[14] Bayle takes somber pleasure in pointing out the primitiveness of the Greeks; he mentions the tradition that Apollo robbed Cassandra of her prophetic powers by the magic use of his spittle (*Continuation des Pensées diverses écrites à un Docteur de Sorbonne à l'occasion de la Comète*). And in his *Dictionary* article on the Thesmophoria, he points out that the noble women of Greece worshiped phalli and the fertility goddess Ceres.

[15] In Bayle's time the materials were beginning to be at hand for a philosophical synthesis of the myths of the dying saviors.

[16] A modern anthropologist has described the important role of self-interested priests in the formation of primitive religion and myth. See Paul Radin, *Primitive Religion* (New York, 1937).

[17] In the paragraphs on Voltaire, I have used for the most part the *Essai sur les Moeurs, Oeuvres Complètes* (Paris, 1878), XI; and *A Philosophical Dictionary*, tr. anon. (London, 1824), especially the articles called "Adam," "Allegories," "Angels," "Annals," "Antiquity," "Apis," "Bacchus," "Emblems," "Fables," "Genesis," "God," "History," "Imagination," "Man," "Miracles," "Moses," "Polytheism," "Prejudice," "Priests," and "Religion."

[18] *Essai*, 1, 42.

[19] *Ibid.*, 35.

[20] *Dictionnaire*, V, 407; and *Essai*, 369.

[21] The most important champions of the astronomical interpretation of myth during the eighteenth century were the Abbé Pluche (*Histoire du Ciel*, 1739) and Dupuis (*Origine de tous les Cultes*, 1795). The latter claimed that Christ, Osiris, and Mithra were sun-gods. Later celestial theories have been advanced by Max Müller (see Chapter IV) and by modern German writers, including Siecke, Ehrenreich, Frobenius, Winckler, and Stucken.

[22] Here he disagrees with Locke and Rousseau—which is partly because Voltaire was deeply impressed by the age-old stability of Oriental societies whereas Locke and Rousseau stressed the more dispersed societies of the American Indians. Locke says that we find the state of nature in "the woods, amongst the unconfined inhabitants that run loose in them." But these "unconfined inhabitants" of Locke's are fictitious.

[23] *Essai*, 20; *Dictionnaire*, IV, 369.

[24] *Dictionnaire*, I, 169.

[25] *Ibid.*, III, 322.

[26] *Essai*, 23.

[27] *Dictionnaire*, V, 406.

[28] *The Philosophical Works of David Hume* (Boston, 1854), IV.

[29] Thus primitive polytheism does not mean to Hume a belief in clear-cut, objectively conceived gods.

[30] I have used a reprint of this book which appeared in 1792 under the title "Fétichisme" in Vol. II in the *Philosophie* section of the *Encyclopédie Méthodique*.

[31] De Brosses thought that fetishism was a universal stage of primitive religion. It is no longer considered an especially important mode of religious worship; it is such a gen-

eralized scheme that the more specific observations which one can make about specific religions are the more important ones. Furthermore, it "appears in typical form only in . . . West Africa." See R. H. Lowie, *Primitive Religion* (New York, 1924), 174. At the time when de Brosses wrote, however, "fetishism" was a salutary and progressive theory.

³² Rousseau repeats the argument of de Brosses: "Man began by animating everything in which he sensed activity . . . the stars, winds, mountains, rivers, trees, cities, even houses, everything had its soul, its god, its life . . . the manitous of the savages, the fetishes of the Negroes, all the works of nature and man were the first divinities of mortals." (*Emile*, ed. by F. and P. Richard [Paris, n.d.], 308.)

³³ The phrase *le monde enchanté* was used by the French translator of Balthasar Bekker's *Die Betooverde Wereld* (Amsterdam, 1691), as the title. During the Enlightenment this book was a standard work on the Devil, who, Bekker proves, does not exist.

NOTES FOR CHAPTER III

TWO PHILOSOPHICAL HISTORIANS

¹ Jules Michelet, *Principes de la Philosophie de l'Histoire Traduits de la Scienza Nuova de J. B. Vico* (Brussels, 1835), 77.

² Benedetto Croce, *The Philosophy of Giambattista Vico*, tr. by R. G. Collingwood (New York, 1913), 46.

³ See Vico's criticism of the Cartesian method in the "Opuscules," *Oeuvres Choisies*, tr. by Jules Michelet.

⁴ The section of the *Scienza Nuova* called "The True Homer" is one of the earliest and most important pre-Wolfian treatments of the Homeric question. Cf. the book of Thomas Blackwell called *An Inquiry into the Life and Writings of Homer* (1735). Already we find in Blackwell the realization that Homer is not a primitive poet and that his poems sprang out of an intricate context of earlier Mediterranean myth. To understand Homer fully, as Blackwell thinks, we must start at a much earlier time, when the Greeks were "a naked company of scrambling mortals." Blackwell's speculations on the influence of climate and natural forces on mythology (cf. also his *Letters Concerning Mythology*, 1748) were to have their effect on Herder—as did the geographical and historical researches of Robert Wood (*Essay on the Original Genius and Writings of Homer*, 1769). It is possible that both Blackwell and Wood had read Vico or knew of his ideas; Herder read and praised Vico. See Introduction to *Vico: His Autobiography*, tr. by M. H. Fisch and T. G. Bergin (Cornell, 1944), 67, 82.

⁵ "Vie de Vico," *Oeuvres Choisies*, tr. by Michelet, 92. Outside the study of myth, Vico was a great admirer of Bacon.

⁶ *Vico: His Autobiography*, tr. by Fisch and Bergin, 171.

⁷ Croce, *The Philosophy of Vico*, 63.

⁸ The dialogue between Mutt and Jute in *Finnegans Wake* is a felicitous transcription of this primitive language, by a writer with an incomparable sense of sound:

Jute: Whysht?
Mutt: The gyant Forficules with Amni the fay.
Jute: Howe?
Mutt: Here is viceking's graab.
Jute: Hwaad!
Mutt: Ore you astoneaged, jute you?

Jute: Oye am thonthorstrok, thing mud.

[9] Croce, *The Philosophy of Vico*, 159 ff.

[10] *Vico: His Autobiography*, tr. by Fisch and Bergin, 170.

[11] The present state of scholarship does not allow us to say whether Hume had read Vico. Fisch and Bergin conjecture that he had, as does J. M. Robertson, *A History of Freethought in the Nineteenth Century* (London, 1910), II, 335; cited by Fisch and Bergin, *Vico: His Autobiography*, 95.

[12] Fritz Strich in his *Mythologie in der Deutschen Literatur* (Halle, 1910) has studied the mythologizing of the German romantics and has shown the great influence of Herder's works.

[13] *Sämmtliche Werke* (Berlin, 1877), I, 444.

[14] *Ibid.*, XIX, 89.

[15] In Germany the most influential doctrines on mythology before J. J. Winckelmann, C. G. Heyne, and Herder were the euhemerism of the Abbé Banier and the allegorical theory of C. T. Damm. Cf. Strich, *Mythologie in der Deutschen Literatur*, I, 8.

[16] *God: Some Conversations*, tr. and ed. by F. H. Burkhardt (New York, 1940); Henry Nevinson, *A Sketch of Herder and His Times* (London, 1884), 338.

[17] *Ideen zur Philosophie der Geschichte der Menschheit* (1783–94), v, 1–3. I have used the translation by T. Churchill called *Outlines of a Philosophy of the History of Man* (London, 1803).

[18] Tr. by Churchill, v, 3.

[19] *Sämmtliche Werke* (Carlsruhe, 1827), XXXVII–XXXVIII, 259.

[20] Quoted in F. McEachran, *The Life and Philosophy of J. G. Herder* (Oxford, 1939), 28.

[21] *Essay Concerning Human Understanding* (London, 1880), 336.

[22] "The Monadology," *Philosophical Works of Leibnitz*, tr. by G. M. Duncan (New Haven, 1908), par. 56, etc.

[23] *Ideen*, tr. by Churchill, i, 3.

[24] *Ibid.*, viii, 2.

[25] The importance of treating Homer and the Greeks anthropologically had been impressed upon Herder by both Blackwell and Wood. They are cited in *Ideen*, tr. by Churchill, xiii. Herder had early pledged himself to the new German school of Higher Critics, of whom he seems most to have admired David Michaelis. Though Herder was a clergyman, he had come to look upon the Bible as a national epic to be studied historically as one studies Hesiod and Aeschylus. The Bible was an Oriental book which contained some of the finest of all poetry.

[26] *Sämmtliche Werke* (Carlsruhe, 1827), XXXVII–XXXVIII, 287.

[27] *Ideen*, tr. by Churchill, xiii, 12.

[28] J. J. Winckelmann, *Thoughts on the Imitation of Greek Works in Painting and Sculpture* (1755); C. G. Heyne, *On the Sources and Causes of Error in Mythological History* (1770). In eighteenth-century Germany, says Strich (*Mythologie in der Deutschen Literatur*, I, 106), "the deepening of mythological knowledge begins with Winckelmann and Heyne and is completed with Herder." Heyne's ideas about the naturalistic origins of speech and poetry and mythical philosophy were closer to Herder's own ideas than were Winckelmann's. De Brosses and his theory of fetishes seem to have been known to Winckelmann and Heyne. The latter observes that "for the moderns, Zeus had no other origin than a fetich." (De la Boullaye, *L'Etude comparée*, I, 237.)

[29] *Werke*, ed. by Suphan (Berlin, 1891), V, 210.

[30] *Decline of the West*, i, 322.

[31] *A History of Ancient Art,* tr. by G. H. Lodge (Boston, 1880), iv, 4 ff.

[32] (New York, 1930), 25.

[33] *Thoughts on Imitation,* cited by E. M. Butler, *The Tyranny of Greece over Germany* (Cambridge, 1935), 46.

[34] *Laocoon,* tr. by Ellen Frothingham (Boston, 1910), 90, 92, 138.

[35] "Erstes Wäldchen," *Laocoon:Lessing, Herder, Goethe,* ed. by W. G. Howard (New York, 1910), xii.

[36] If to Winckelmann myth was hardly different from noble allegory (see his *Versuch einer Allegorie,* 1766), to Lessing it was a form of revelation. Lessing outlined his somewhat cryptic theory in his *Erziehung des Menschengeschlechts* (1780). Myth, he thinks, is the form which the revelation of divine truth takes in the early history of nations; myths are not, to be sure, "truths for the reason"; but they are metaphors or allegories revealing potential truths. Myth takes three forms: (1) "a preliminary exercise"; God's threat to the Jews to punish even the third and fourth generations for the sins of their fathers was a preliminary exercise in the doctrine of immortality; (2) a "sign" or "hint," i.e. an oblique expression which is a "germ . . . out of which a truth still withheld may develop"; for example, the phrase "God of Abraham," intimating the coming of Christ; (3) "an allusion"; in other words, a metaphor such as "to be gathered to his fathers" which God used to excite the curiosity of His people.

These mythical forms appear in allegories of events which are thought actually to have happened, e.g. the origin of evil is told in the story of the tree and the origin of tongues in the story of Babel. The style of myth, he tells us, is simple and poetic, and myth is a national "primer" in its "positive perfection." This being so, he warns against too philosophical and intricate interpretations, against "shaking allegories empty."

[37] This is Herder's later conception as expressed in the *Ideen.* At this time he was much impressed by reports of the idyllic societies of the South Seas. His typical Dionysian feeling is somewhat softened in this late work.

[38] "Erstes Wäldchen," *Laocoon,* ed. by Howard, 208.

[39] *Fragmente, Werke* (Berlin, n. d.), I, ii, iii.

[40] *Ibid.,* i. Herder's theory of language resembles the more mystical one of Hamann, under whose influence Herder came in his early days. Herder agrees pretty well with Vico on the mythopoeic character of early languages, though his idea of poetry is more sentimental than Vico's. Rousseau's idea of linguistic evolution was strikingly Viconian. His idea that a mythological word and a realistic word were likely to be attached to the same object, the first in a state of terror and awe (when the object appears unfamiliar) and the second in a calmer, more rational state (when the object appears familiar), is suggestive to students of myth. See the "Essai sur l'Origine des Langues," *Oeuvres Complètes* (Paris, 1835), III, 495.

[41] Tr. by Churchill, viii, 2.

[42] *Ibid.,* v, 1.

[43] "We remember the fish which we did eat in Egypt freely—the cucumbers and the melons and the leeks and the onions and the garlic—but now our soul is dried away." Num. 11:6.

[44] *Sämmtliche Werke* (Carlsruhe, 1827), XXXVII–XXXVIII, 227.

[45] *Vom neuern Gebrauch der Mythologie, Sämmtliche Werke,* (Berlin, 1877), I, 441.

[46] *Sämmtliche Werke* (Berlin, 1877), XV, 535.

[47] *Ideen,* tr. by Churchill, viii, 2.

Notes for Chapter IV

MYTH, HISTORY, AND PHILOLOGY

[1] Otfried Müller, *Histoire de la Litterature Grecque*, tr. by K. Hillebrand (Paris, 1883), I, 3.

[2] *Über die Encyclopädie der Alterthumswissenschaft*, cited by Hillebrand, tr., *Histoire de la Litterature Grecque*, I, 45n.

[3] Andrew Lang, *Homer and the Epic* (London, 1893), 20.

[4] *Kleine Schriften*, II, 842.

[5] If the student of myth were to follow his subject into the realms of German idealism, he would have to consider the nature symbolism of Hegel (*Philosophie der Weltgeschichte*) and the more complicated theories of Schelling. Schelling is much concerned with Dionysus, the spiritual force who liberated the human mind from slavery and made mythology possible. The mythology of the Greeks was a frustrated poetical attempt of the human spirit to achieve "pure freedom" and the ultimate revelation of a transcendent God. This revelation, an eternal process, was given to mankind by Judaism. Schelling's theory has the virtue at least of seeing mythology as a necessary function of human culture. See Schelling, *Philosophie der Mythologie und Offenbarung*; V. Jankélévitch, *L'Odyssée de la Conscience dans la Dernière Philosophie de Schelling; Schelling: Of Human Freedom*, tr. and ed. by James Gutmann; and Schelling, *The Ages of the World*, tr. and ed. by F. de W. Bolman.

Creuzer and Schelling represent that branch of romantic thought which from the Greeks down has always tried to translate mythology into a system of recondite wisdom. In this sense they are akin to the Neoplatonists of all ages. They must be carefully distinguished from the more pragmatic romantics like Vico and Herder, who are far better students of myth. In this connection, we shall later try to distinguish between mythology and "paramythology."

[6] On the whole, I have followed Otfried Müller's interpretation of Creuzer. See Otfried Müller, *Introduction to a Scientific System of Mythology*, tr. by J. Leitch (London, 1845), 268 ff.

[7] See his *Antisymbolik* (1824) and the earlier *Mythologische Briefe*. Cf. Otfried Müller (Leitch, tr.), *Introduction*, 259 ff.

[8] *Briefe von Hermann und Creuzer* (Heidelberg, 1818), 15–16. The philological controversy of the time has been treated by Ernst Howald, *Der Kampf um Creuzers Symbolik* (Tübingen, 1926). Renan discussed this controversy in "Les Religions de l'Antiquité," *Etudes d'Histoire Religieuse* (Paris, 1864), objecting to the spiritual "refinement" and penchant for symbolization which Creuzer attributed to primitive peoples.

[9] First published in 1825.

[10] The opinions of George Grote, who was well versed in German philology, are still interesting. Grote is resolutely skeptical. Myth is "a special product of the imagination and feeling, radically distinct from both history and philosophy." He finds Otfried Müller "full of instruction." But he thinks myth can never be shown to be even in part historical. Even the myths concerning the siege of Troy must be regarded as purely imaginary. Creuzer he believes to be entirely wrong; so far as we can show, there is no symbolic philosophy in the ancient myths. Myths are made philosophical only in later periods by individual thinkers whose scientific understanding sets them apart from the people, while

the thought of the people remains entirely mythopoeic. Though far less rich and suggestive, Grote's idea of myth is similar to that of Vico, whom he calls "an eminently original thinker" and quotes at length. See *History of Greece*, I, 341, 343, 434, 435, 436, etc.

11 "Mythologie comparée," *Nouvelles Etudes d'Histoire Religieuse* (Paris, 1899), 31, 35.

12 *Chips from a German Workshop* (New York, 1869), I, 1–141.

13 For such objections, however, see the evidence assembled by Andrew Lang, *Modern Mythology* (London, 1897), a reply to Max Müller's *Contributions to the Science of Mythology* (London, 1897). On the same subject see Lang, *Custom and Myth* (London, 1893), 45, 64, 87. Lang's researches convinced him that there was agreement among the philologists on the names of only two of the Olympic gods: Zeus and Demeter. Lang, *Myth, Ritual and Religion*, II, 295.

14 *Contributions*, I, 113.

15 *The Science of Thought* (London, 1861), I, 322–23.

16 *Chips*, II, 77.

17 *The Science of Thought*, I, 212.

18 Max Müller's theory—traditionally called the theory of *nomina numina*—has a long pedigree. Palaephatos (2d century B.C.) used it in interpreting myths, as did John Selden in the seventeenth century (*The Syrian Gods*, 1617). The theory also appeared in C. G. Heyne's *De causis fabularum* (1764) and his *Sermonis mythici* (1807). In *Chips*, II, 140, Max Müller objects to Heyne's strict idea of the *poverty* of human speech and says that primitive speech is at once impoverished and poetically rich.

19 On Max Müller's questionable opinion about the etymology of "Endymion," see E. S. LeComte, *Endymion in England* (New York, 1943), 34.

20 *Modern Mythology*, 11–19.

21 *Ibid.*, 140.

22 *Chips*, II, 56.

23 *Ibid.*, 72

24 *Contributions*, I, 51.

NOTES FOR CHAPTER V

THE ENGLISH RATIONALISTS

1 *Primitive Culture* (London, 1871), I, 281. Unless otherwise noted, all the citations of Tylor are from the three chapters on mythology in this book.

2 *Ibid.*, 417 ff. To Tylor, "animism" was "the minimum definition of religion." This theory is now generally thought to be too exclusively intellectual. It does not adequately account for the religious emotions, or for those primary ideas of preternatural power variously designated by savages as *mana, orenda, maxpé*, etc.

3 Hume could have taught Tylor something about the pragmatic purposes of such magical activities!

4 J. M. Robertson traces Tylor's theory of animism back to Hume and Vico (*History of Freethought in the Nineteenth Century*, II, 359); but this is misleading: both Hume and Vico made pragmatic judgments about primitive psychology. Tylor's rationalist point of view had more in common with treatises like Adam Smith's "Principles which Lead and Direct Philosophical Inquiries as Illustrated by the History of Astronomy," *Essays* (London, 1890), 325 ff. Smith derives mythology from a primitive science of nature.

5 Max Müller, *Chips*, II, *passim*.

6 "We are too apt to argue as if the psychical conditions of the earliest men were exactly like our own," wrote Andrew Lang in his *Modern Mythology;* "while we are just beginning to learn from Prof. William James, that about even our own psychical condition, we are only now realizing our exhaustive ignorance."

7 *Primitive Culture,* I, 31.

8 See *Principles of Sociology* (New York, 1923), I, 412–34, 830–41, 842–49.

9 *Modern Mythology,* xii. All other citations of Lang are from *Myth, Ritual and Religion.*

10 *Sociology,* I, 404.

11 Lang's opinion has been applauded in later times by apologists of religion (Schmidt [Rose, tr.], *Origin and Growth of Religion,* 172 ff.), but also by American anthropologists (Paul Radin, *Primitive Man as Philosopher* [New York, 1927], 345: "Lang's . . . intuitive insight has been abundantly corroborated.") Radin believes, however, that the high god was less an object of tribal worship than a philosophical idea entertained only by intelligent individuals. See his *Primitive Religion,* 259. R. H. Lowie's *History of Ethnological Theory* (New York, 1937) supports Lang's idea; see 83.

12 *Primitive Culture,* II, 361.

13 It is important to consult the 3d edition (1906) of Lang's *Myth, Ritual and Religion,* which differs radically from the first edition (1887). Between editions he had set forth his theory of the high god in *The Making of Religion* (1898).

14 Lang's evidence is primarily Australian, though he also adduces the African Bushmen, the Hottentots, and the North American Indians. Between the publication of Tylor's *Primitive Culture* (1871) and 1906 the Australian tribes had become much better known (cf. the reports published by A. H. Howitt, and Spencer and Gillen). Lang considered the Australians "the lowest known savages"; they are now considered more culturally complex than the Andamanese, the Fuegans, the California Indians, and others (Lowie, *History,* 206).

15 The question is from Menzie, *History of Religion,* 23. The rest of the quotation is from *The Making of Religion,* 281–82.

16 Sir James Frazer is of the company of English rationalists. But in all the vast range of his books we find no important theoretical positions which we have not already met in Tylor, Spencer, or Lang, though Frazer's emphasis on vegetation rites and myths may be traced to Mannhardt (*Wald- und Feldkulte,* 1875; etc.). Frazer is always unhappy in the presence of theory. When Lévy-Bruhl's theory of the "prelogical" savage comes to Frazer's attention, he cries, "Enough of these fantasies. Let us return to the facts." And this is typical of his attitude.

Gilbert Murray and Jane Harrison (the latter is the author of *Themis,* 1912; *Prolegomena to the Study of Greek Religion,* 1922; etc.) are two other representatives of the school of Hellenist-anthropologists in England. Originally they took the theoretical positions of Frazer and pictured Dionysus, for example, as a vegetation god and Greek tragedy as a rehearsal of the annual death and resurrection of the vegetation. They soon tempered the rationalism of their English predecessors, however. Miss Harrison, like Murray's son-in-law A. J. Toynbee, found a more mystic meaning in Greek religion after she had come to understand the philosophy of Bergson. E. Durkheim also came to figure in Miss Harrison's thought and the gods of Greece became projections of communal emotions.

Durkheim perhaps deserves more attention than we can give him here. The interpretations of religion set forth in his *Elementary Forms of the Religious Life* (1910) are admired in part but rejected as general theory by the American anthropologists. Reacting sharply against the English rationalist psychology, as Comte before him had reacted against

Cartesian psychology, Durkheim rejects individual psychology almost completely (again like Comte) and supposes that religion is an immediate product of the social group; religion is a social *mystique* and is to be studied as sociology. This mystical strain also appears in another member of the French School, Lucien Lévy-Bruhl. In his *How Natives Think* (1926), he set forth the notion that primitive thought is prelogical and mystic, that primitive man has no conception of the simplest logical rules of cause and effect or of contradictory fact, but lives in a world where everything is fused into a "mystic participation" with everything else—and hence that primitive thought is different *in kind* from civilized thought, a fundamental position which the American anthropologists do not accept (by "American anthropologists" I mean in general those who came under the influence of Franz Boas at Columbia: see Chapter VI).

NOTES FOR CHAPTER VI

MYTH AND MODERN ANTHROPOLOGY

[1] Cf. e.g. Ruth Benedict, *General Anthropology* by Franz Boas and others (New York, 1938), 630; R. R. Marett, *The Threshold of Religion* (London, 1914), 281–82.

[2] P. 9.

[3] *Primitive Religion*, 14.

[4] Paul Radin, *Social Anthropology* (New York, 1932), 269.

[5] Though Lowie's *Primitive Religion* is primarily a psychological study and neglects socio-economic determinants, the author insists on the great influence of "theologically-minded castes," 63. And he observes that among the ordinary Crow Indians "the greater or less dignity of the shamans depended solely upon the pragmatic test of their efficacy," 14.

"Shaman" is a Siberian word indicating a religious leader whose neurotic or epileptic propensities have made him the recipient of hallucinatory trances and thus made him the object of general reverence. Other distinguishable religious leaders are the medicine man and the priest. I shall usually designate these three types of religious leader by the general word "priest" or "priest-thinker."

[6] *The Golden Bough* (abridged ed.; New York, 1940), 11.

[7] *Ibid.*, 49.

[8] *Tylor* (London, 1936).

[9] Agreed upon by Benedict, *General Anthropology*, 630; Lowie, *Primitive Religion*, 147; A. A. Goldenweiser, *Early Civilization* (New York, 1926), 246–47.

[10] *Mana* was first described by R. H. Codrington, *The Melanesians* (Oxford, 1891).

[11] "The Fundamental Concept of the Primitive Philosophy," *The Monist* (1906), XVI, 357–82.

[12] *General Anthropology*, 631.

[13] Professor Benedict uses the word "supernatural" after making the necessary qualifications upon it. Where she uses "supernatural," I use "preternatural."

[14] *General Anthropology*, 629.

[15] *Primitive Religion*, 14.

[16] *The Threshold of Religion*, 9, 22.

[17] *General Anthropology*, 630.

[18] *Primitive Religion*, 5.

[19] *Ibid.*, 23.

[20] Radin, *Social Anthropology*, 262.

[21] On the problems of cultural selection, consult Ruth Benedict, *Patterns of Culture* (Boston, 1934).

[22] A. A. Goldenweiser, *Anthropology* (New York, 1937), 443 ff.

[23] Benedict, *General Anthropology*, 634.

[24] *Primitive Religion*, 75. The reader of N. Söderblom, *Das Werder des Gottesglaubens* (Leipzig, 1916) and R. Otto, *Das Heilige* (Gotha, 1926) will be familiar with this attempt to identify religion by means of one instinctual emotion. This kind of study attained a considerable vogue in the twenties.

[25] R. Fortune, *The Sorcerers of Dobu* (New York, 1932); Benedict, *Patterns of Culture*, 130.

[26] Radin, *Social Anthropology*, 326; *Primitive Religion*, 260; *Primitive Man as Philosopher*, 303.

[27] This ancient and profoundly erroneous opinion is by no means extinct. It is maintained by the folklorist Joseph Campbell in the appendix of his edition of *Grimm's Fairy Tales* (New York, 1944).

[28] *Art as Experience* (New York, 1934), 30.

[29] Franz Boas, *Race, Language, and Culture* (New York, 1940), 406.

[30] *Ibid.*, 420, 454.

[31] The Winnebago tale called "Brother and Sister" related by Radin, *Social Anthropology*, 357–58. Lowie has pointed out that the heroes of American Indian mythology, who retire to some dark or unearthly realm to undergo a test of strength, are only secondarily and spasmodically related to the setting and rising sun. R. H. Lowie, "The Test Theme in North American Mythology," *Journal of American Folklore*, April–September, 1908. Cf. the Arthurian heroes.

[32] *Race, Language, and Culture*, 480.

[33] Lowie, *Primitive Religion*, 21.

[34] *Race, Language, and Culture*, 405; Ruth Benedict, "Myth," *Encyclopedia of Social Sciences*; R. H. Lowie, *The Crow Indians* (New York, 1935), 111; and indeed almost any modern American anthropologist; as well as the English folklorist E. S. Hartland, *Mythology and Folktales* (London, 1914), 34–35.

[35] *General Anthropology*, 589.

[36] Consult the voluminous publications of the American Folklore Society and the English Folklore Society. Also the exhaustive *Motif-Index of Folk Literature* by Stith Thompson (*Indiana University Studies*, XIX–XXIII, 1932–36).

[37] *Apollodorus:The Library*, tr. by J. G. Frazer (London, 1921), xxvii.

[38] *The Frazer Lectures* (London, 1932), 66–120.

[39] Boas, *Race, Language, and Culture*, 455.

[40] Goldenweiser, *Anthropology*, 408.

[41] *Race, Language, and Culture*, 504.

[42] *La Mythologie Primitive* (Paris, 1935), xxiv.

[43] *Race, Language, and Culture*, 454.

[44] *Ibid.*, 405.

[45] *Grimm's Household Tales*, tr. by Margaret Hunt (London, 1913), II, 579–80. Introduction by Andrew Lang.

[46] In a note to *The Lady of the Lake*, cited by Lang in *Grimm's Household Tales*, tr. by Hunt, xli.

[47] *Chips*, I, 243.

[48] *Grimm's Household Tales*, tr. by Hunt, xli–xlii.

[49] *Mythology and Folktales*, 34.

50 *Elements of Folk Psychology,* tr. by E. L. Schaub (New York, 1916), 270, 387.

51 *Art as Experience,* 19.

52 Goldenweiser, *Anthropology,* 425.

53 *Primitive Man as Philosopher,* 246.

54 *The Threshold of Religion,* 15.

55 *Essay on Man* (New Haven, 1944), 76.

56 *Experience and Nature* (New York, 1929), 96. Cassirer cites this passage: *Essay,* 76.

57 "We rightly speak of the magic of art and compare the artist with the magician." Sigmund Freud, *Basic Writings,* tr. by A. A. Brill (New York, 1938), 974.

58 Cf. William Butler Yeats's "The Second Coming":

> Things fall apart; the centre cannot hold;
> Mere anarchy is loosed upon the world.

59 If we define metaphor as the figurative fusion of two (or more) activities, the present discussion obviously raises the question of the relation between metaphor and myth. Vico thought, as we have seen, that "every metaphor is the abridgement of a fable." This is true if we specify the two active worlds which the metaphor fuses as the preternatural and the natural and then select, among metaphors which do this, those which operate as myth does. We might notice in passing that the practice of magic must have been a powerful influence in conditioning the aesthetic psychology to metaphor and simile. This is because of the endless analogies the magician makes between his own mental and emotive processes and the external activities of the world, and between different objects. As Professor Benedict writes, "practically all the similitudes in nature have been employed somewhere in the magic of some people" (*General Anthropology,* 639).

A symbol may perhaps be described roughly as a precipitated metaphor, as crystals are precipitated out of chemical solutions. Vico was right to insist that myth is not primarily symbolic. He is amply supported in this opinion by modern anthropologists such as B. Malinowski ("Myth in Primitive Psychology," 73) and Radin (*Primitive Man as Philosopher,* 209). Primitive art uses symbols: all art does. But the symbol is something likely to be read by commentators into what was created by the fluid play of the imagination. A pointed interest in the use of symbols is not so characteristic of savages as it is of semanticists.

60 Benedict, *General Anthrolopogy,* 640.

61 *Reason in Religion* (New York, 1916), 57.

62 *Threshold of Religion,* 114.

63 Benedict, *General Anthropology,* 660.

64 Lowie, *Primitive Religion,* 85.

65 *Race, Language, and Culture,* 482.

66 Citations in these paragraphs refer to Radin's *Primitive Religion,* unless otherwise noted.

67 Freud writes (*Basic Writings,* tr. by Brill, 878): "While magic retains the full omnipotence of ideas, animism has ceded part of this omnipotence to spirits and thus has started on the way to form a religion. Now what could have moved primitive man to this first renunciation?" To this question Radin furnishes an answer which would not be likely to occur to Freud: i.e. "the priests and economic necessity." For Freud's answer, see Chapter VII.

68 I first understood magic and religion in this manner from reading Radin's *Primitive Religion:* see 7 and *passim.*

69 Cited in Frazer, *Apollodorus,* xxiv.

[70] L. R. Farnell, "The Value and the Methods of Mythologic Study," *Proceedings of the British Academy* (1919–20), 44.

[71] *Apollodorus,* xxvi.

[72] Goldenweiser, *Early Civilization,* 333.

[73] Radin, *Social Anthropology,* 316.

[74] Radin, *Primitive Religion,* 49, 53.

[75] Radin, *Primitive Religion,* 68.

[76] *Race, Language, and Culture,* 401.

[77] *Primitive Religion,* 196.

[78] Benedict, *Patterns of Culture,* 68.

[79] *The Golden Bough* (London, 1913), IX, 386.

NOTES FOR CHAPTER VII

MYTH AND PSYCHOANALYSIS

[1] *Basic Writings,* tr. by Brill, 974.

[2] *Ibid.,* 876; *Beyond the Pleasure Principle* (London, 1922), 5.

[3] *Basic Writings,* tr. by Brill, 497.

[4] Freud leaves this idea somewhat vague. He does not accept the fantastic Jungian hypothesis of a "collective unconscious" into which primitive thought is eternally plunged and into which we regress in our dreams, art, and neuroses, cf. Jung's essay called "Mind and Earth," *Contributions to Analytical Psychology* (London, 1928), 110. Jung's theory involves a belief in "the racial memory," according to which the general experience of mankind is recorded in the "collective unconscious." This idea certainly overestimates the conservatism of the psyche and of culture. Ruth Benedict observes that the study of folklore gives no hint of a racial memory; see *Zuni Mythology* (New York, 1935), xiv. Many dreams can be shown to take their form and meaning from the cultural environment. Like myths, they are made *ad hoc* and disappear when there is no more use for them—whereas if there were a racial memory, we should expect dreams to be preserved and stereotyped therein; see J. S. Lincoln, *The Dream in Primitive Culture* (London, 1935), 24.

[5] *Basic Writings,* tr. by Brill, 906.

[6] Quoted by Freud, *ibid.,* 925.

[7] *Early Civilization,* 396.

[8] "Totem and Taboo in Retrospect," *American Journal of Sociology,* November, 1939.

[9] Freud himself is diffident about "Totem and Taboo" as history. Perhaps, he reflects, the primeval parricide has only a "psychic reality" (*Basic Writings,* tr. by Brill, 929). Elsewhere he refers to "Totem and Taboo" as "a scientific myth"—see *Group Psychology and the Analysis of the Ego* (London, 1922), 112.

[10] Different societies seem to employ different methods of guarding against the Oedipus neurosis. Cf. Benedict, *Patterns of Culture,* 101.

[11] *Sex and Repression in Savage Society* (New York, 1927), 81.

[12] *Basic Writings,* tr. by Brill, 807.

[13] *Primitive Culture,* II, 49.

[14] *On the Nightmare* (London, 1931), 274.

[15] Lincoln amasses considerable evidence, but he seems to me to be too eager to make anthropology conform to psychoanalysis.

16 These technical words are explained in the chapter called "The Dream Work" in Freud's *Interpretation of Dreams*. (London, 1922).

17 Otto Rank, *The Myth of the Birth of the Hero*, in *Nervous and Mental Disease Monograph Series* (New York, 1914), no. 18, p. 7; Karl Abraham, *Dreams and Myths*, same *Series*, no. 15, *passim*; Carl Jung, *The Psychology of the Unconscious* (New York, 1931), 29.

18 "The Horse and Infantile Sexuality," *On the Nightmare*, 273 ff.

19 *Psychology of the Unconscious*, 160 ff.

20 *Myth of the Birth of the Hero*, 5. The German "Pan-Babylonians" took up the torch from the Aryan scholars. Employing much the same methods, they transferred the Primitive Paradise from India to Babylon and tried to show that the mythologies of Greece, Israel—and perhaps of all the world—originated in the astrolatry of the Babylonians. (H. Winckler, *Himmels- und Weltenbild der Babylonier*, 1903; E. Stucken, *Astralmythen*, 1907.)

21 *Basic Writings*, tr. by Brill, 361–63, 398, etc.

22 *Dreams and Myths*, 13.

23 Cf. Benedict, "Folklore," *Encyclopedia of the Social Sciences*.

24 *Basic Writings*, tr. by Brill, 543.

25 *Ibid.*, 315–20.

26 Cf. Wordsworth's dream of the phantasmal Arab, discussed in Chapter VIII.

27 E. g. Lowie, *Primitive Religion*, 12; Lincoln, *The Dream in Primitive Culture*, 87.

28 *Beyond the Pleasure Principle* (London, 1922), 5.

29 "Myth," *Encyclopedia of the Social Sciences*.

30 Nevertheless, we might recall that even dreams are functional. Freud describes the dream as "possessing intrinsic value as psychic action," as being "a psychic act full of import." Dreams perform the function, as Freud insists, of preserving sleep, just as, in the largest sense, we have described myth as preserving wakefulness. (Cf. *Basic Writings*, tr. by Brill, 282, 485, 209, 287.)

31 (London, 1927). In these paragraphs, however, I use the simpler essay called "The Anatomy of the Mental Personality," *New Introductory Lectures on Psychoanalysis* (New York, 1933), 82–112.

32 *Basic Writings*, tr. by Brill, 183.

33 *Ibid.*, 543.

34 The dream censor is described both in *The Interpretation of Dreams* and in *New Introductory Lectures*, though in the latter work Freud thinks of the dream censor as one activity of the more comprehensive superego. See Lecture xxix.

35 "The Winnebago Tribe," *37th Annual Report of the Bureau of American Ethnology* (Washington, 1923), 225, 285, 287, 316.

36 One is nearly tempted to think of the Transformer as a projection of the psychic process which changes the latent content of the dream into the manifest content—the process which Freud calls "the work of transformation" (*Basic Writings*, tr. by Brill, 467).

37 *Race, Language, and Culture*, 473.

38 *Ibid.*, 414.

39 *Ibid.*

40 We must admit that the dream censor is not a very clear conception. Freud best described it by comparison with the political censor of newspaper editorials; and perhaps all I have been able to do here is draw an analogy between the censor and the priest, though I admit I have tried to suggest a relationship closer than analogy.

We must remember, furthermore, that Freud believed dream censorship to be "alto-

gether different, qualitatively, from waking thought" (*Basic Writings*, tr. by Brill, 467).
But it would surely be surprising if such an influential trait of the human psyche were
confined to one area of human experience.

[41] "The 'Uncanny,' " *Collected Papers* (London, 1925), IV, 368–406.

[42] Preface to "The Beast in the Jungle," *The Great Short Novels of Henry James* (New
York, 1944), 751.

[43] When T. S. Eliot does not read extraneous theological meanings into it, his idea of the
"objective correlative" of poetry conforms with what Freud says about intellection in
dreams. In a "philosophical" poet—Dante, for example—Eliot does not find philosophy
but its "emotional equivalent."

[44] *Basic Writings*, tr. by Brill, 543. See also 361, 404, 423, 433, 434.

[45] "The Legacy of Sigmund Freud: Literary and Aesthetic," *Kenyon Review*, Spring,
1940.

NOTES FOR CHAPTER VIII

THE LARGER VIEW

[1] *Reason in Religion*, 51.

[2] "Paramythien? Was bedeutet das Wort? Paramythien heisst eine Erholung . . . sie auf
die alte griechische Fabel, die Mythos heisst, gebauet sind und in den Gang dieser nur
einen neuen Sinn legen." Herder, *Werke*, ed. by Suphan, XXVIII, 127.

[3] *Elements of Folk Psychology*, 51.

[4] (Harvard, 1942). I have quoted 36, 149, 150, 151, 158, 201, 203.

[5] In support of this judgment on primitive thought, Mrs. Langer cites E. Cailliet. But
Cailliet is of the French sociological school which, like its leader, Lévy-Bruhl, imagines
savages to be in a perpetual trance (see E. Cailliet and J. A. Bédé, "Le Symbolisme et l'Ame
primitive," *Revue de Litterature comparée*, April–June, 1932). Mrs. Langer often depends on Gilbert Murray and Jane Harrison for opinions about primitive thought. But
why these French mystics and old Edwardians when the American anthropologists are full
of such glad tidings?

[6] "Magic," *Essays* (London, 1924), 51.

[7] The critical method of Professor Douglas Bush, *Mythology and the Renaissance
Tradition in English Poetry* (Minneapolis, 1932), and *Mythology and the Romantic
Tradition in English Poetry* (Harvard, 1937), leads him to slight much of the best
mythological poetry in English; for example, some of the seventeenth-century metaphysical
poetry and the poetry of Blake. We should expect him to slight Wordsworth (who is allotted fourteen pages to Shelley's forty). "The poetry of his great decade," writes
Professor Bush of Wordsworth, "certainly contains very little mythology in comparison
with his later and generally inferior work." Yet it must seem to anyone who finds some
degree of truth in the definitions of myth we have been trying to set forth that Wordsworth wrote in his great decade some of the best mythological poetry in English, and that
there is far less of the mythical in his later poetry than there is in his earlier.

[8] *Social Anthropology*, 358.

[9] *Race, Language, and Culture*, 449.

[10] Benedict, *Zuni Mythology*, xiv.

[11] The reader will perceive from the general argument of this book that my method
would be the same if I were considering other kinds of literature. For example, Bantu

legends, Grimm's *Fairy Tales,* a detective story by Dashiell Hammett, a popular tale about Benjamin Franklin, or *Superman.*

[12] *English Institute Annual, 1941* (New York, 1942).

[13] This passage and certain other passages on poetic psychology are more enlightening to students of myth than the parts of Bk. iv of *The Excursion* which explicitly concern myth.

INDEX